ALL THINGS NEW

The author on holiday in Cornwall, in August 1964, when this book
was written.

ALL THINGS NEW
A Declaration of Faith

By

Anne C. Biezanek

HARPER & ROW, PUBLISHERS

New York and Evanston

FIRST AMERICAN EDITION

LIBRARY OF CONGRESS CATALOG CARD NUMBER: 65-14689

CONTENTS

To Ben Greene, my Quaker father,
without whose wisdom and loving guidance
I would have lost my way.

And to Jan, my own true Pole,
who, in this cause, has endured much. . . .

ACKNOWLEDGEMENTS

My thanks are due to all the Roman Catholic writers who have contributed to my understanding of 'The Faith', and who receive no specific mention in this book.

Next must I thank Peter Smith, without whose original encouragement and unfailing enthusiasm I would never have embarked.

For the references to authorities on medieval history, I am indebted to my father, Ben Greene, who delved freely for me into his great stores of knowledge.

To the Reader:

In view of all the press publicity I have received, this book has to be written.

I am writing under pressure. Clearly, the mother of a large young family who has to run a home with very little domestic help has literally no leisure. In fact, without the whole-hearted co-operation of a truly remarkable mother, who has her own home to run in Scotland, none of the activities in which I am engaged would be possible.

Therefore, do not look for polished writing or the well-turned phrase. This book simply pours forth under its own momentum, with every word coming straight from the heart.

Then I saw a new heaven, and a new earth. The old heaven, the old earth, had vanished, and there was no more sea.

And I John saw in my vision that holy city which is the new Jerusalem, being sent down by God from heaven all clothed in readiness, like a bride who has adorned herself to meet her husband.

I heard too, a voice which cried aloud from the throne: 'Here is God's tabernacle pitched among men; he will dwell among them, and they will be his own people, and he will be among them, their own God.

'He will wipe away every tear from their eyes, and there will be no more death or mourning, or cries of distress, no more sorrow; those old things have passed away.

'And he who sat upon the throne said, "Behold, I make all things new. . . .".'

THE APOCALYPSE OF THE BLESSED APOSTLE, JOHN.
Chapter 21, verses 1–5 (*Knox Version*).

PART ONE

CHAPTER I

THE BACKGROUND TO THIS BOOK

I AM on holiday once again in the same remote little North Cornish fishing village, staying in my mother's holiday cottage, where we have come every summer of my life. This year I am here with my mother and seven children, as I was last year and the year before that and the year before that. Nothing has changed, the same sun blazes down on the same glorious golden beaches fringed by the same towering cliffs. When the gales blow in from the Atlantic, the same doors rattle and the same windows leak and the same lamps smoke.

Through the years the number that has arrived to take up its monthly sojourn in the cottage has increased, as the size of the family has increased, until now there are nine of us. The pattern of our arrival, our sojourn and departure has remained the same. But this year there are additions to the luggage – a typewriter and a suitcase full of letters.

In the eleven short months that have passed since our departure last year, and our arrival this year, I have been transformed from a quite unknown and insignificant member of the medical profession to a figure of international interest. The suitcase contains hundreds of letters, these being but a selection of the hundreds and hundreds that have been pushed by the sackful through the door of my home in Wallasey, since the beginning of this year.

What is it that has prompted so many people to write to me, and to write in such moving and intimate terms, to me a stranger? They have read in their newspapers that I, a Roman Catholic doctor, have opened a birth control clinic in my own home, and for so doing have suffered a public rebuke at the hands of the Church Authorities. The reporting by the national press of this simple sequence of events seemed to act as a spark that triggered off a chain of explosions in the minds of thousands, not only in this country, but all over the world, wherever the news was received. I have letters from Canada, U.S.A. and Mexico, from the Philippines and Pakistan, from Australia, New

Zealand, South Africa and Rhodesia, from Holland and Germany and Italy and France, from Cyprus and Japan and Sweden and Poland, from countries I have never been to, in languages I do not know, from men and from women, from Roman Catholics and Methodists and Anglicans and Presbyterians, from Jehovah's Witnesses and Quakers, from Buddhists and Moslems, from Humanists and Communists.

These letters are frequently addressed simply to: 'The Roman Catholic Birth Control Clinic, Liverpool, England', or 'Dr. Anne Bieżanek, The Clinic, England', and they all seem to reach me (thanks to our wonderful Post Office!). Wherever possible I have answered every one of these, both from home and abroad, though in some cases I have failed, due to inadequacy of translating facilities, or to the pressure of too great a number.[1] To those who wrote to me and received no reply, I would like to say now, 'Thank you, your letters were marvellous, they have meant more to me than words can say. Through them I have been enabled to retain my sanity and humanity, which otherwise I would have lost.'

For I have been caught up in a machine that is inhuman in its workings, and seems to care not at all for the welfare of the individual soul. I mean the machinery which governs my own Church, the Most Holy Roman Catholic Church.

All this has burst upon me since last I was here. But even as I write, the children are tumbling out of their beds, down the cliff and into the sea and I must pause in my writing and make the breakfast porridge.

What is it exactly that has led me to write this book? It is nearly eight years now since my difficulties with my own Church began and led to my first nervous breakdown. I struggled and prayed my way back to sanity. A sanity based more and more upon my experience of reality itself.

When the news of my activities reached the ears of the world, I had already done all my basic thinking. I had decided that the enormity of the evil that was being perpetrated through the mechanism of a spiritual totalitarianism had to be resisted. I knew that the strength required to make this resistance had to come from resources within myself.

[1] Grateful thanks are due to the International Planned Parenthood Federation for generous help with translation.

I was in a way in the same position as those Germans who had found themselves enmeshed in Nazism and who had come to realise that Nazism was not good. Their choice lay between running away, denying all responsibility for the evil they had themselves been partly responsible for, or making a stand then and there and saying out loud: 'These things are wrong.'

It is fashionable to have very little sympathy for those Germans who failed to follow either course, but continued to muddle along to the end, an end that proved so very bitter indeed. We say that they *ought* to have stood their ground and suffered. We say that such willingness to accept individual responsibility and its consequences in inescapable suffering is the only way a repetition of the Nazi horror can be avoided. And yet it is marvellous how many otherwise responsible people seem to see no analogy in the issue of spiritual totalitarianism.

The Roman Catholic hierarchy, finding that they cannot silence me, might well wish that I would transfer my spiritual allegiance elsewhere. But it is surprising how many non-Catholics whose advice I originally sought expressed this same view. 'The Roman Catholic Church is too powerful for any individual to stand up to,' they would say. 'You ought to quietly leave that Church, as so many others have been obliged to do before you.' In other words, I was on all sides advised against that very course of action which we expected Germans to take under Hitler, and indeed hanged them for failing to take. If Nuremberg means anything, it must mean that no man is safe from the wrath of his fellow men, and judgement day, on this earth, awaits us all. Let all take heed of this, for none shall escape.

So as this conflict with my spiritual overseers increased in intensity so did my determination to stick it out to the end, no matter what the consequences. For if I could be ground down so mercilessly and have my personal problems treated with such contemptuous disdain, so could all my fellow Catholics suffer likewise; very few of whom were likely to be as well equipped as I in physical and educational resources.

But during the whole course of this conflict I was working entirely in the dark and quite alone, and without the slightest reason to suppose that any of my fellow Catholics did have these same troubles with the Church. Catholic relations and friends, to whom I explained my problems, took the line that my very difficulties were proof of my lack of sincerity as a Catholic, and were 'sent' as punishment for hidden sin. Thus was Job comforted in days of old.

So when the issue broke upon the public I had no reason to suppose that Roman Catholics would not despise me for it, and non-Catholics conclude that I was simply 'touched'.

But I was not to be kept in suspense for long, for following hard upon the first press report came the first letters. These letters, as well as the telephone calls that poured into my home like a heavenly benediction, all said the same thing: 'YOU HAVE DONE WELL.' G. K. Chesterton wrote a poem, the refrain of which is 'we are the people of England, we have not spoken yet'. In January 1964, when total disintegration of personality faced me, the people of England spoke to me and told me that all was well. And then followed the messages from overseas. Here I must give my thanks to the much maligned press of this country. The reporters who have sought admission to my home, have shown themselves, without exception, to be dedicated and sincere men, not looking for the sensationalism that might have ruined me, but wanting to understand and help. That these same men might behave differently in a different context only serves to show how real and desperate they know this problem to be.

Some extracts from a tiny handful of these letters I give here. They are not given in an attempt to show that I am a person as marvellous as the writers sometimes suppose, for let it be remembered that not one of these people has ever met me. For an assessment of the sort of person I really am, let my own family, who have to live with me, speak. I can assure all readers that such an assessment would not prove so idyllic. No matter, the people who choose to see me in the light they do are merely giving vent to an emotion that has been suppressed until it has reached fever pitch. Seeing nothing but hypocrisy, darkness and downright lying in the contemporary Roman Catholic scene, they saw my stand as a message from heaven, no less than that 'God has visited His People'.

So, therefore, with no further apology to offer, I present these extracts – but with one comment that I wish all to take note of now: I have had quite as many letters from men as from women, and some of these, written by men, are the most beautiful of all received, so imbued with love and understanding that they should serve as the complete antidote to the unfavourable assessment of that sex that I had hitherto formed, but which I regret must still show forth in subsequent writings in this book. My own thinking is based on an experience of the male sex that is not, on the whole, flattering, and that is history and I cannot alter it. Time and more favourable experience alone can work a cure.

LETTERS

(1) *From Catholic Women*

'. . . The best years of my married life have been difficult, sometimes unhappy, my temper has suffered and I would not wish the same experience to my daughter . . . so add this voice of encouragement to your fight. . . .'

'. . . I am the youngest of a large family, I have never forgotten that my mother said "I would not wish my worst enemy the sufferings of a large family", so you can see how she suffered. . . . It seems to me that Christian idealists are often one-sided and the cost of their ideals . . . falls heavily on women . . . in self-defence they must resort to contraception. . . .'

'We are two catholic wives and mothers who are in full agreement with the stand you have taken. We would like to say how much we admire your tremendous courage in dealing with this long overdue problem. . . .'

'Please don't give up your good work, I was born and reared a Catholic and my husband is a convert. We have four children. We realise we can't go on having children, so last year I got the Pill . . . my conscience is quite clear. . . . I believe the church will accept it one day and I think you may be the one to make them see this. . . . My marriage nearly broke up at one time through this and I thought "Which would God rather see, a broken home or a happy one?" and I know I have the right answer.'

'After a good few years' spiritual starvation – not receiving the sacraments – I have at last resolved my own problem, but for the sake of those who have not and are in dire need of your help, God give you strength. . . . Living in close harmony as a man and wife do, one cannot remain united with this fear always with one. . . . Your spiritual starvation will be the worst thing to bear. God give you strength. . . . Remember this is a woman's fight. . . .'

'I am a woman of few words. . . . I felt I must tell you that I am with you all the way. . . . Good luck and God bless you. . . . My heart goes out to all the unwanted and neglected children . . . would love to help you in your work. . . .'

'You have made public a problem which has haunted women secretly for many a long year. . . . It is a great relief to know that one is not alone in questioning the Church's teaching on birth control. I could write pages and pages on my feelings on this matter, but I know you fully understand the hardship it causes. . . .'

'I am a Catholic mother in the 6th month of my 7th pregnancy and would like your advice. . . . I feel my nerves are in tatters, I seem unable to cope with children. . . . Surely God in his wisdom, does not mean homes to be broken. . . . I thought perhaps I was the only one in the world with a problem like this. Sometimes I think I am unstable when I can't face up to any more of it. . . .'

'I am a Catholic mother – aged 65 with 13 adult children – and two who died. My fight is over, but I am deeply concerned for the spiritual welfare of my family. . . . Please keep up your efforts. . . . I hope your own children will in time understand and thank you. . . .'

'I think it is only the laity, and particularly Catholic women, who will induce the Fathers to revise their teaching. . . . Let's hope and pray that it will be in our generation. . . .'

'I know only too well how you feel being a Catholic myself with the same ideas . . . the conflict is great in one's mind, but once you come to terms with it and feel in one's heart that one is right, then there is no need to worry about any one else. . . . I had a nervous breakdown, the conflicts with my religion had a lot to do with it. . . .'

'How right you are in the campaign you are leading. I can only speak from my own bitter experience, which is that I am expecting my 10th child in November (the oldest sixteen) and have had complications with every single one. . . . I now feel so desperate that my view at the moment is that death is preferable to life. . . . May you be successful against these obsolete ideas. . . .'

'The fact that a R.C. woman has had the courage of her convictions and gone ahead with actions as well as words, is more than I would have dared hope for. . . . I am so grateful to you. . . . Don't EVER close your clinic, no matter what. . . .'

'Then the fits started again . . . my memory is still defective . . . it's always worse when I'm pregnant . . . my husband still won't use any method of birth control so I have to go behind his back. . . . I have four children, all "safe-period" ones . . . so my life is sheer misery. . . . My husband won't even discuss any other method . . . results are I don't go to church. . . . When I see all these Catholic families with two or three children, so nicely spaced, I wonder how they do it. . . . I spoke to the priest and said I wanted to practise my religion and needed help, he told me not to be sorry for myself, and not to listen to my doctor. . . . I have just told my husband I am going to the F.P.A. clinic and now he won't speak to me.'

'As a Catholic mother, I am writing to say how much I admire the wonderful work you are doing. . . . We use contraceptives and so do all my Catholic friends. Please carry on the good work. . . .'

'Hundreds and thousands of Catholic women must now be silently blessing you, as well as the parents of Protestant children who have married Catholics. . . .'

'As the mother of seven expecting her 8th at the age of 31, I feel very strongly that a person should be allowed to follow his own conscience. . . .'

'I am a nursing sister, Irish, Catholic, aged 57. . . . I pray that your sufferings and troubles may bring you where He who permitted them and honoured you with them, intended our sorrows in this life to bring us – to the light and glory of our own real home. . . .'

'Our Church is so bound up with man-made laws and red tape, that in many instances God's love and understanding is barred or hidden from those who seek the love and happiness He longs to shower on those who search for Him. . . . God will never fail you, maybe your work will not be any the less, but at least you will enjoy such peace of mind that all else will seem trivial. . . .'

'If only there had been someone like you 60 years ago. I lost my dear aunt in childbirth. She was only 32, and left a baby of 3 hrs. old – her seventh. Seven motherless children to be deprived of a living mother who had lost her vitality and strength in child-bearing too quickly and abundantly. . . .'

'How very apt to have dedicated your clinic to St. Martin de Porres, the friend of the unfortunate. Who is more unfortunate nd friendless than the thousands of Catholic women who suffer through the church's teaching on birth control. . . .'

'As a Catholic girl who has been advised, for health reasons, not to have any children, I am going through a very trying ordeal. . . . I can fully appreciate your difficulties from a professional point of view, and I should like you to know that my prayers are behind you. . . .'

'I am wanting to tell you how sorry I am for the trouble you have and to congratulate you on having the courage of your convictions. . . . I always remember you in my prayers and offer my holy communions for you. . . .'

'As an R.C. mother of six children, I wish to thank you for the work you are doing and the hope you are bringing to our over-worked mothers, for whom the "safe-period" does not work. . . . So far I have found little charity from our clergy. . . . We say our family rosary every evening and for the month of May will offer it for you and your work. . . .'

'It is time there was a suffragette movement in the church, for the freedom of Catholic women to plan their families in the safest way . . . every success to you.'

'I am an Irish R.C., I have two children, I have practised birth control all my married life and never confessed this to a priest, as I firmly believe I am doing right. . . . I am confident that your good work can only bring happiness to millions of married people. That God will understand you . . . and your reward will be great. . . .'

'As a deeply sincere Catholic mother, I feel I must write and congratulate you on your work. . . . I myself use a diaphragm contraceptive . . . do not think it is a sin, and am quite right to continue my sacramental life. I feel as you do that we Catholic mothers have a duty to "stand up and be counted" on this issue. It is too important to leave to silence, to time, to the individual conscience. . . . I am immensely grateful for your courage. . . .'

'I am a Catholic with 8 children, after my last child was born three years ago my husband and I decided to practice birth control. . . . Since then we have not been to the sacraments ; . . but we attend Mass and try to bring up our children as good Catholics. Are we to remain for ever "lepers" because we now have some happiness together as a family. . . .'

'I am a Catholic mother of 13 children, now all grown up . . . the church has now accepted the theory of family planning. It must follow this up by serious discussion by clergy and lay people who have the right of personal experience or it is going to be faced with the problem of more lapsed or indifferent Catholics.'

'I am an S.R.N. . . . for the past few years have been torn between religious confusion and bitterness arising out of being constantly pregnant. . . . I feel as strongly as you do on this matter, and I know other Catholics who do too.'

'I feel, like other R.C.s, that there is no scandal attached to your case at all.'

'Like yourself I am very proud of my religion and beg you to continue this work, whatever may be demanded of you. God alone knows the heartache, anguish and mental torture that can and does come in married life, when just a little common sense and understanding is all that is needed. . . . Every Sunday I offer my communions for you. . . . Stand firm, dear Doctor, the hopes of millions rest with you, and the relief of untold suffering. . . .'

'My husband and I are R.C. but neither of us have received communion for 5 years because we practise birth control. We go to mass every Sunday but feel like hypocrites. . . . I believe a great deal of R.C.s practise birth control as we do and receive the sacraments. . . .'

(2) *From non-Catholic Women*

'Mothers with growing daughters will be firmly behind you in your efforts for happier family planning. The young people themselves will pray for God's own blessing on your very worthy aim.'

'If more Catholics would take a stand as you have done I am sure the Catholic church would have to change on this issue. . . .'

'What does it matter if the whole world is against you, if you are right with God. . . ? You are the Lamb against the Lion, but your faith in the powers that God has given you will not fail you, as the church has done on this issue.'

'Permit me to express my appreciation of your courageous effort against those who would seek to destroy your God-given liberty of conscience, thought and action.'

'You have not gone against God no matter what man may say. . . . Your battle is against sin and ignorance, the Lord is behind you to the full. . . .'

'I am writing to say how much I hope you will carry on with your work and have faith in your convictions. If you give up now, it will be all the harder to bring about birth control for all faiths. You are keeping alight a candle which must illuminate the minds of all men. . . .'

'For the sake of your church, the greatest service you can do for it is to proceed serenely with the work you feel that God has given you to do. . . .'

'I feel your fight is for all women, and would like you to know how much I admire you, and that I remember you in my prayers. . . .'

'You are just wanting to do as HE, our dear Saviour, commanded you to do. Who are they, the heads of the greatest political establishment in the world . . . to tell you that you cannot take communion, unless you follow their instructions . . . so, go my dear, and take Communion, Praise the Lord, and He will dwell in your heart and bless you mightily.'

'I speak as a qualified and practising midwife, when I say that I have seen the physical condition of women worn out with repeated child bearing . . . advised by their doctors to undergo sterilisation operations, and yet having to endure the most terrible mental conflict because it is against their religion. . . . I pray that you may find peace of mind and comfort from the grateful thanks of the women you treat, and the marriages you must undoubtedly save. . . .'

'Please stick to your guns, you are a brave woman. No church that rules by fear is worthy of the name. . . .'

'I am just an ordinary housewife and member of the Church of England, but I have studied the R.C. faith. I believe in spacing a family. . . . I pray that you will have faith, not just to take communion, but for strength, if and when refused. Jesus will send His Holy Spirit and enter your heart and give you His peace, and the Peace of God will give you the patience and strength to carry on.'

'. . . how can you be wrong to prevent the sickness of broken homes spreading still further? How can you be wrong in struggling with the chains of injustice? How can you be wrong in defending the right of man? How can you be wrong in defending the right of God? . . . It is only wrong for the church. Instinctively you know you are right, instinctively the down-trodden Catholic mothers know you are right but you have the moral courage to say so, and whatever action the church might decide on, you cannot escape the fact that you defended the right of man and God, when you accepted this challenge. How can you lose? You can live without the church, but you cannot live apart from your conscience. . . . The sacraments that the church takes from you will be restored by God, if you defend what is right. You are much nearer to God in this respect than the church gives you credit for.'

'I admire the stand you are taking to reduce the mental anguish of ordinary folk, who when leading clean and decent lives, are always afraid, and wait anxiously every month. . . .'

'How much I admire your courage in going ahead with your scheme to start a family planning clinic. To quote your own words "I believe I have been sent by God to give the clergy a shaking. . . ." Yes, I believe you have. . . . It seems to me that the main issue at stake is the dignity of human life. . . .'

'I hope I will live to see the day when a Higher Domestic Science paper will have a question on the role played by Dr. Anne Bieżanek in liberalising the R.C. church to birth control, its effects on raising the status of women and on family life in the latter half of the 20th century.'

'I am a widow and have had 10 children, and wish I had known more about birth control when I was young. . . . I dreaded each pregnancy, we were always poor . . . and much unhappiness was caused by being afraid of intercourse.'

'I was one of a family of 11 and it was terrible for us, also for our mother who was dragged to the grave child by child. . . . There is no Christianity about that kind of thing, it is more like the works of the devil. . . . There will be plenty to condemn you Dr. Anne, but saints in the bible were also condemned, so do not give up, there are women in England and the whole world who need your help.'

'Do not let the withholding of the sacraments worry you. You are doing a good Christian work, which being full of compassion and charity for your fellow creatures, has the blessing of Almighty God. The Judgement on the immensely rich churches has already been pronounced by God Himself: ". . . Inasmuch as you did it not unto the least of these my brethren, you did it not unto me." '

'I am not a Roman Catholic, but suggest that all Christians read the bible for themselves and not just listen to man without proving their religion to themselves. Sincerity is not enough to please God. . . .'

'The community as a whole owes a great deal to such courageous people as yourself – and your fellow Catholics, some of whom cannot understand your point of view, will one day realise it too.'

'Catholic women everywhere will thank you for the step you have taken. . . . I think it wrong to leave this matter to the discretion of men.'

(3) *From ex-Catholic Women*

'No doubt you have had many bricks thrown at you but this is a bouquet. Words cannot express the admiration I feel for you. . . . I was a practising Catholic . . . what appalled me was the fact that most of my friends used methods against the ruling of the church but just kept quiet about it and still continued going to church, no one had the guts like you to make a stand. . . .'

'There is no doubt in my mind that the time has come to make this protest from within the church, and I am equally certain that you have been chosen to make it. I pray that you will not suffer too much – but I am confident that you are prepared to.'

'The idea of a God so dictatorial was inconceivable to me, and I left the church some years ago. . . . I was luckier than most, and have found, at last, an intelligent and humane God, through Quakerism.'

'If only you had been born sooner! What a lot of misery we women would have been saved. . . . My mother had 18 children, 12 of whom lived(?) in hunger and for the most part barefoot and ill-clad. If only she had been given the knowledge that you, in your God-given wisdom, can give to us women. . . . I think a woman should not have to face the awful dread of becoming pregnant in order to keep her husband's love, and the marriage together. . . . Just speak to God yourself, as I have had to learn to do, and ignore the "good" people who dare to refuse you the holy sacraments.'

'I was a Catholic, educated at a convent school, but did not marry in the Catholic faith . . . having 5 children quickly . . . my health and nerves suffered. During one operation I was refused confession and communion with marrying a non-Catholic. . . . I have had my own views since . . . and no-one now can alter them. They fill the world with unwanted children, whom some neglect and others ill-treat, so why not family planning? Women died for the vote and women's emancipation. This only needs women with brains believing in what is right.'

'You are sent by God on a most sacred mission. . . . Would Christ let women suffer so? It is blasphemous to think He would agree with the R.C. church.'

'I pray God will give you the strength and support to match your courage, don't falter now, this goes much deeper than religion. I am a grandmother aged 52. I lost a wonderful mother, she died aged 41, leaving 11 children, in childbirth. . . . I remember my father's remark, when the doctor pleaded with him: "It's not Christian to use birth control" . . . slowly we saw our dear mother crucified . . . birth control would have saved our family, our mother, our home, our happiness. . . . My husband is mentally ill, due to the hardships he suffered as a member of a large family and a selfish father. . . my life has been hell at times because my husband resented the sheath I encouraged him to wear. . . . I was often in danger of being strangled because of it. . . . A pill would have improved our health and relations with each other.'

'I was received into the Catholic church from the Church of England to marry a Catholic man . . . when expecting my third child my husband was unemployed and we had 30/– a week to keep four of us . . . with three children I refused to have any more, as I said it was a greater sin to produce children you could not afford than to take precautions . . . my husband refused for "fear of hell" . . . after years of frustration, tension, physical and mental illness, our marriage broke up. . . . I am thankful my three daughters married non-Catholics, who are not ruled by the man-made laws of the R.C. church . . . which make millions of people frightened and miserable and I think are worse than the Gestapo, as they kill souls rather than bodies. . . .'

'I am the eldest daughter of 22 children and miscarriages. These my mother had up to the age of 40. Her life and especially the lives of the older children were just hell. My father was a drunkard and the physical and mental cruelty he inflicted on my mother, even during pregnancy, and on us children is unbelievable and the horror of my early life has never left me. My father was a Roman Catholic and we were too, but as I became older I became convinced that no woman should be used as my mother was used. . . .'

'Fifteen years ago I had to struggle with my conscience over whether or not to use birth control and in desperation sought the advice of my parish priest. His intolerant attitude, his unsympathetic manner and complete lack of understanding of a problem that was getting too big for me, caused me to have a complete mental breakdown, because I was torn between loyalty to my husband and loyalty to my religion, and my husband is a good husband. . . . I did a lot of thinking. The way the church teaches makes her inhuman to the rights of others, because it is human to err. Her treatment of you is not human, her treatment of me was far from human. . . . The celibacy of her teachers is not human and is an example mankind cannot follow . . . and it puts them in a position where they cannot practise what they preach. . . . I have taught my children truth by always telling them the truth and I shall never go into a Catholic church again while she continues to exalt herself, because this is not Christ's teaching. . . .'

'I was born and educated a Roman Catholic . . . but have not practised my religion since I decided to use birth control after the birth of my son 12 years ago. . . . This has had a far more far-reaching effect than it sounds. . . . Catholics do not know the meaning of truthfulness, as I know and have argued with several who practise birth control, without confessing it to a priest and who still regard themselves as paragons of true Catholics.'

'I should like to express my admiration for your single-handed battle for Catholic women. . . . I was a Catholic mother and became pregnant through the church's suggestion of the "safe period". I had the baby and a severe mental breakdown . . . the cost in healthy emotional development to my other children is incalculable, as I was ill during their formative years. The cost to the Health Service during this illness must have come to several hundreds of pounds. All this could have been avoided if the Church had permitted modern methods of birth control. And I am just one isolated case. During my psychiatric treatment I came to see how wrong and damaging the Catholic policy is, and I changed my religion. I am now a Quaker and I also practise effective birth control. The change in our lives has to be experienced to be believed. . . .'

(4) *From Catholic Men*

'May I, a sixty year old man, express my admiration of your desire to help your fellow human beings. The Catholic church is wrong to condemn you, you are doing a brave job and all sensible people know and recognise that fact. Carry on as you have started, you will find friends, real ones. One cannot deny that the domineering hold of the churches is decreasing and common sense prevailing. So God bless you Doctor and don't worry about a thing.'

'I am aware that it is politically feasible for the church not to waver. If the change comes it must come from within and its coming will be ponderous and laboured, but you have set an example and a leader has been thrown up from the masses. May you be successful.'

'I am quite sure you are going to be one of the pioneers of this step forward into family happiness, and the people who now are trying to demoralise you will end with their faces red.'

'Though I am a strict Catholic, from a strict Catholic home, and a strict Catholic college, there are some rulings in the Church that I cannot reconcile myself to. . . . Good luck and God bless you. . . .'

'I am a convert to the faith and I feel this teaching to be quite out of touch with modern ideas. . . . I hope you can convince those in authority of the common sense of your ideas.'

'I would like to congratulate you on your determined stand on birth control. I am a Catholic and if I was refused communion under similar circumstances, I would not worry.'

'I am the father of three children and my wife and I cannot partake of the Blessed sacrament and have not done so for years, for the same reason that you are in difficulties . . . you have the support of a great number of us.'

'My wife and I believe your stand to be the most worthwhile thing in the world today.'

'As a married man and father of two children, I applaud your courage in confronting the high priests as you are doing.... We too have used contraceptives with a clear conscience and still attend communion, feeling certain that we are doing no wrong. Please do not lose heart, we have long needed someone like yourself. You are doing more for christian unity than a hundred priests.'

'Congratulations on your wonderful fight for what you believe . . . rest assured there are millions of Catholics with you . . . you will be remembered in many people's prayers. . . .'

'They have no right to stop God entering your soul, if you wish Him. They have no right to deprive you of his body and blood. Who do they think they are? They are supposed to be God's servants, not His Advisers! To me you are a better Catholic, nearer to God than those "saintly" priests that refused you the sacrament. Do remember Doctor the priests didn't create our religion and although they should uphold it they are making a poor mess of it sometimes. Remain a Roman Catholic Doctor, we could do with more like you.'

'As a staunch Roman Catholic myself . . . I believe with more than two kids we couldn't exist on our income, as it is we are not living just existing. . . . I am a student. . . . We can't go to communion as we practise birth control and without it we would have four kids, and only two rooms to live in and no food to eat. . . . I am, I suppose, a critical case as far as a young Catholic's faith and future is concerned and as I am so young, some advice would do me good. . . . I was longing to get someone to talk with who could discuss things with no partiality. . . . I feel really upset to realise that I am opposing the church. . . . I could never tell my parents. . . .'

'I am 21 years old and not married, but I do admire you for sticking up for the rights of Roman Catholics to happiness without fear. . . .'

'I'm a Roman Catholic born and bred in Dublin but I don't see what right those priests have to criticise the good and sensible work you are doing. Why not deprive those drunken layabouts of husbands, who give their wives a baby every year, of the sacraments and leave a good kind woman like you alone?'

(5) *From non-Catholic Men*

'I wish to express my moral support and admiration for your courage in following your conscience in the face of certain reactionary men who claim to know the law of God but to me seem the modern counterpart of the scribes and pharisees.'

'I imagine I am old enough to be your father, but my admiration for your determination and courage in maintaining your principles in the face of the opposition you have encountered, is so sincere that I felt I must write to you.'

'Remember that all intelligent and real christians are solidly behind you and it is not necessary for you to explain or defend your position. Don't let any one worry you.'

'I admire women for many things applicable to that sex. They work long hours and put up with many inconveniences without complaining, something that men would not tolerate. On top of this, to ask them to bear children once every 12 or 24 months reduces them to slavery. . . . Men as a sex are selfish, as far as they are concerned their one thought is self-satisfaction, and as one who lost a mother at 54 worn out with having 10 children, I feel that something should and ought to be done about it in this day and age. . . .'

'Do not fall into the trap that Martin Luther fell into when he made a gentleman's agreement to leave the Papacy alone if the Papacy left him alone.'

'I am not a Catholic, I am also a mere man, but I wish you and your sisters every success in your fight to decide your right to have or not to have children. . . .'

'I cannot tell you how much I admire your courage in standing up for what you believe in against a doctrine that has caused untold misery in this family. Your opening of a family planning clinic shows courage equal to a Battle of Britain pilot. . . .'

'What I do know is that when we are called to account for our stewardship in this life, your courage will stand out like a shining beacon – sacrament or no sacrament, the Almighty will say: "pass friend – all is well" and I am proud to think that I know when I hear of such a splendid woman.'

'I do not suppose there is any need for me to tell you to keep on fighting as you are a woman of great courage whom I admire tremendously . . . in fact I admire you so much that I will stand by you in a literal sense and do battle with you. . . . I will write to you again and again if necessary if it helps you even a little not to weaken, and to keep faith in what you are doing.'

'As an ordinary layman I send greetings to you. . . . I wish you every success in your work . . . to educate the community, which to my mind is a Christian contribution to society. May you long continue. . . . I am a Methodist and worship the same God as you do . . . and I know His abundant love is about, because there are many ordinary people who are loving you and praying for you at this time.'

'As an ordinary working husband, I wish to thank you for the good work you are doing, to prevent suffering and misery to parents and little children alike, born and unborn. . . . Your action makes you a good christian.'

'. . . your name will and should go down in history . . . you are a woman who cares. . . .'

'The time is coming when the Christ-being, working through countless thousands selfless ones, will sweep away all insincere tradition, hypocrisy, lies and half truths . . . and will place in the hands of the good, sincere and kind, the government of the world. . . . God be with you. . . . I send you all my admiration and strength I can and would help in any way I could.'

'I am sure that what you lose in the eyes of the Church you gain in the help you are able to give to the people round about you. . . . I am the Father of ten children . . . after a few years I found out that four of my boys and a girl had muscular dystrophy and after a time all five had to be in wheel chairs. . . . My wife passed away during an operation, that was seven years ago. I have kept my family at home . . . two of my boys have passed away . . . my wife was a wonderful person and a good wife and mother . . . she would not practise any sort of birth control or allow me to and I do think that by having so many children she was unable to stand this strain of a major operation. I do hope this letter will help you carry on with your good deed. . . .'

'I am a committed Christian, a believer in the Lord Jesus Christ with a faith real and down to earth, and like Him realising the importance of love and compassion to one another. I have no intention of sermonising, but I would encourage you to endure for the sake of others in your care . . . for His love was and is the practical well being of individuals. . . . I have always admired women of strong character and purpose and believe me, without flattery, I admire you.'

'The church burned Joan of Arc and after many years made her a saint, and the conduct of the church is no pattern. May the God of all parts inspire you. . . .'

'God has given you a mission to fulfil, a great ideal, a Christian ideal, a glorious ideal in helping to give all that is good to human life. Would Jesus the saviour say that He wanted to take you off the servant's rolls? No, He would say "Go to thy labour of love for my people" so dear Doctor take up your cross and follow in His footsteps and He will give you the strength to carry on. . . . He cares, He loves, He ordains your work as a blessing to all. . . . I am 81 years old and a member of the church of Jesus Christ.'

'. . . I would like to make the further point. If the bishop decides to excommunicate you [AS HE HAS] does God have to say "very good Bishop, I'll do as you say and cut her off"? . . . to act against your honest convictions is, I am sure a much greater sin than displeasing a bishop. . . .'

It would seem that the position I had taken up on birth control, in my own little corner of Wallasey, did in fact coincide with a vast unrest in the whole Roman Catholic world. Catholic writers were becoming more outspoken, and even from the closed ranks of the clergy were heard isolated noises, as of ice cracking. . . .

In the middle of May, I was asked by *The Scotsman* to submit an article on my views. Up to this time, though quite a lot was being written *about* me, I myself had written nothing. About the same time I was invited by the Rotary Club of Birkenhead to give a talk on 'Roman Catholics and birth control'. I went along and gave my talk about this and that and found my audience most charmingly enthusiastic. So I asked them if they thought this matter on which they had heard me speak would make a suitable article for *The Scotsman*? They said they thought it would, and that I ought, most emphatically, to write it. So home I went and the talk was put to paper and posted to Scotland, where it was published on May 26th, 1964. In this article I outlined my ideas on the need for the definition of a new dogma – that of the co-redemptrix, and attempted to show how the solution to the birth control controversy in the Roman Catholic church must centre around and become in itself dependent upon this definition. This was the theme that the Rotarians of Birkenhead had enjoyed hearing me expound. This was the theme of the article that *The Scotsman* so generously published. In the brief flurry of published correspondence that followed, it appeared that some Catholic women in Scotland were not impressed. They did not like my ideas on the need for contraceptive practice in marriage, and they did not like my theological assertions. 'Who is this woman and who does she think she is?' was the prevailing tone of the letters that appeared. My mother, who lives in Scotland, though not herself a Roman Catholic, was nevertheless following the matter with some interest, and submitted the following letter that was published on June 3rd.

SIR – I wonder if the mother of Dr. Bieżanek might be allowed to answer Mrs. Robertson, who accuses my daughter of a 'mass of verbiage, ignorance and woolly thinking', etc.

My daughter married while still at Aberdeen University. She had two sons by the time she took her finals, five children by the time she sat her Diploma in Psychiatric Medicine, and seven children living and eleven pregnancies in all when her first child was only 13. Some of this time she was in a full-time job as registrar in a large mental hospital.

She had a breakdown.

When she felt at the end of her tether she wrote to various priests begging for advice and help. One actually wrote that this was her cross, she must not withstand her husband but she was assured a place in heaven. She was to have a heavenly reward, and her children could be scattered into Homes. . . .

I am not a Catholic, but in my daughter's dire need, when she was faithfully following the teaching of her Church, not one single Catholic came to her rescue. We her parents did. But this gave her furiously to think, for thousands of women would not have parents able or willing to do what we did. And this was when she began to see the Pill as God's answer.

In her marriage vows she undertook to be a helpmate to her husband and to bring her children up as good Catholics. She must keep well to do this. And surely it must be clear to the meanest intelligence that rhythm methods or total abstinence can only be mutually achieved. No priest was ever able to suggest how this could be enforced.

(Mrs.) LESLIE M. GREENE

It seemed to me that this approach of my mother's was realistic and helpful towards bridging the chasm that would appear to exist between my present theological orientation and that of other members of my Church. So many Catholics simply cannot understand what it is that I am saying.

When it came to writing this book, the need for which was being cautiously suggested by friends, Catholic and non-Catholic, it seemed to me to be necessary to start the book with an account of my own vicissitudes, spiritual and otherwise. It is these that have led me on to the development of my clinic on the one hand and to the development of certain theological ideas on the other. Both of these manifestations of my own understanding of the Roman Catholic faith seem to strike a note of somewhat startling originality to the minds of the uninitiated. To try to meet this dual difficulty, I have kept the book in two major parts. One concerned with 'ME' and the hard facts of life with which this 'me' has had to contend, and the other consisting of a statement of my present thinking in relation to Roman Catholic doctrine as a whole.

CHAPTER II

THE BACKGROUND TO MY
RELIGIOUS FAITH

I WAS seventeen years old, away from home, frightened, mixed up, and miserable. I developed on my own, strange and, some would say, morbid interests.

My imagination was fired by Poland, poetry, and the Roman Catholic religion. In that order.

The war was just over and I had heard some people I knew commenting, with great distress, on 'The Polish Settlement'. 'A nation betrayed,' are the words I heard. 'The very nation for whom we went to war!'

Thus I stood at the threshold of my University career, staring at the recent revelations of the German concentration camps, frightened and without comprehension. 'Why?' was the question. 'Why did this happen? Is it going to happen again?' I began to consider the accumulation of bitterness that had led to these culminating horrors – the concentration camps and the atom bomb. These matters formed the first serious concern of my awakened adolescent consciousness. I did not want to get blown up by an atom bomb, nor did I want to die in a concentration camp. Particularly did I not want that.

Thus my earliest desire to put wrongs right was based, quite frankly, on a desire to survive. If no one were to kill me horribly, then I must make sure that no one had cause to want to. Thus my earliest efforts to do good were based on the fear of the consequences. 'Do good' is perhaps overstating the case. Rather was it a desire to see justice done, not justice for its own sake, but that amount of justice that would still hatred, because hatred is destructive, and I feared it.

Now that my attention had been drawn to Poland's fate, I was filled with fear. I remembered that it was for Poland and Justice that we had gone to war. The sound of Polish soldiers singing as they marched through Aberdeen echoed in my heart. I knew her to be one of our victorious allies.

Now some terrible shadow had fallen. Eyes dropped when Poland was mentioned. It became easier, less embarrassing, not to mention her at all.

What of the future? Could my sense of internal stability as a British subject be secured on the basis of such a blatant injustice?

We had gone to war to save Poland. We had not saved her. Her armies suffered defeat. She was partitioned between her enemies and used as a battle-ground by them. Polish soldiers who escaped we were glad to accept as allies. We had encouraged a secret army to develop in Poland under the noses of the Germans. We watched this army wage one of the most terrible battles of all time: the Battle of Warsaw 1944. During the course of this battle the Russians stood across the Vistula and watched. . . . They watched for thirteen weeks; they watched the Germans move in ten armoured divisions; they watched the city, Poland's heart, torn into shreds; they watched indeed the murder of the Polish nation. They watched with grim quiet. They watched until the last Polish soldier had been blown out of the last sewer. They then began their own assault on the city. The city they captured from the Germans was a total ruin.

From the Russian point of view, their action was very prudent, and they may well be commended for the efficiency of their manoeuvre. When the Russians demanded that Poland be added to their newly-acquired empire, they were acting in the manner they had always said they would act. In this at least they were consistent.

Did we hear America protest? No. . . . She acceded so readily to this rape of a nation; it was almost as though the Statue of Liberty in New York harbour was not only blind but deaf too.

And Great Britain, poor Britain, with strength enough for but a feeble, ineffectual protest on behalf of her erstwhile ally! Not a decade before that same ally had precipitated Britain into a world-wide war, fought on the principle that might cannot make wrong right. Could it be that now the British people thought that if an injustice was ignored for long enough and studiously enough it would perchance disappear as the memory faded?

Put forward whatever argument you like to explain the

British and American attitude to the Polish settlement, but do not ask anyone to believe thereafter in the justice of the West's cause against Communism.

In our abandonment of Poland we lost sight of justice, we acted according to expediency in relation to a friend who had trusted in us. In this we lost faith in ourselves. Was not this symptomatic of our times? A dissolution of those high ideals with which we were wont to flatter ourselves. Could honour, could justice be allowed to bow to expediency?

The whole discreditable episode disturbed me deeply. I felt ashamed for my country. It would have been a poetic retribution for England herself to suffer the same bloody rape as Poland, at the hands of communised Poles. I found myself thinking this. It was unhealthy. So to escape the thought I strove for a more constructive approach, if only for my peace of mind.

Sir Winston Churchill had stated publicly his belief that the Polish settlement was 'just and right'. The statement still stands. This statement can only be comprehended in one sense: a betrayal of trust cannot be just or right; nor was the crucifixion just or right, when looked at from the highest earthly standards. Yet when looked at through the eyes of God, we are told by theologians, the Crucifixion *was* just and right. In the same sense I was able to accept Poland's fate as just and right. In that sense alone was I able to bear the spectacle.

The Polish mystical poets of the nineteenth century had seen in their visions that Poland's national spirit would overcome all adversity, and this spirit they came to identify with the Holy Ghost himself, the Second Person of the Blessed Trinity. This Person is referred to by them as Poland's *Spirit King*.

I found this daring concept echoed in the poem by G. K. Chesterton entitled 'Poland'. He states that the sign, raised for ever in that heroic land, shining 'terrible as the Holy Ghost' is *'an Eagle whiter than a Dove'*.

The white eagle is Poland's national symbol. The dove is the symbol of the Holy Ghost. In a flash of prophetic insight this great Englishman saw the Polish national emblem, transplanting the dove, as the symbol of the Holy Ghost. For, mark well, the eagle of his vision was *whiter* than the dove. The tremendous implications of the message contained in this simple line of poetry captivated my mind when I was still but seventeen years old, and I had never exchanged a word with a Pole in the flesh. And I can truthfully say that this concept has dominated my thinking ever since, even though I have by no means always understood its implications.

At the same time I was deeply and powerfully moved by another poem by another man, who though not exactly English had an English mother, and wrote in English: Hilaire Belloc. He wrote of the spiritual implications to himself brought about by a pilgrimage to Chęstochowa, Poland's national shrine. This monastery has figured greatly in Polish history, and houses a painting of the Virgin Mother of Christ, of great antiquity, and believed, by Poles, to possess miraculous powers.

Belloc pinned his poem to the wall beside the picture, where it remains, presumably to this day, along with countless thousand other such offerings. In this 'Ballade to our Lady of Chęstochowa', Belloc includes the following verse,

> Steep are the seas and savaging and cold,
>   In dark waters terrible to try,
> And vast against the winter's night the wold,
>   And harbourless for any sail to lie.
>   But thou shall lead me to the lights, and I
> Shall hymn thee in a harbour story told.
> This is the faith that I have held and hold,
>   And this is that in which I mean to die.

In the eighteenth century this picture was crowned by the Papal envoy in a ceremony that dedicated the Polish nation to Mary, in a sense that I think no other nation is so dedicated. The present Polish Peoples Republic still has a crowned Queen. This Queen is also known as the Queen of Heaven.

Thus, I had in my spiritual sights a nation that had the Holy Ghost for its uncrowned King, and the Mother of Christ for its crowned Queen. That the issue of this royal union MUST be Christ Himself seemed to me self-evident. Christ in that particular role of 'redeemed nation-hood', of which the Polish poets had already written.

If I am asked to state more precisely what I mean by 'Christ revealed through a nation redeemed' my answer is: I do not know yet what I mean, but simply watch the Polish nation, and you will see the mystery unfolding before your eyes.

Anyway, to get back to me: I was now eighteen years of age and thinking all this; what could I do then and there for Poland? Clearly nothing. She was in the hands of her enemies. But somehow I felt that this enemy willed her good, in a sense that the Germans never did, nor are now capable of doing. The Russians have never hated the Poles just for being Poles, in the sense that the Germans have, and to a certain extent still do. Nor does Communism, as an ideology, hate any nation for itself. Rather did I gather, from the Communists I met at the University, that Communism sought universal justice, and sought it at a somewhat deeper level than the comfort of the individual non-Communist would permit him to recognise.

But I could also see that Communism alone was not sufficient. It did not take into account that sense of national destiny that was an essential part of my vision. Rather did I see Communism itself breaking her teeth on this particular nation, and in the process undergoing a transformation.

At this point I began to think more deeply about the Roman Catholic religion. That alone seemed able to give some coherence and permanence to this somewhat nebulous mass of highly charged material. At eighteen I was without any formal religious beliefs, had no 'moral code' to lean on, and was all but blinded by the splendour of the thoughts that assailed me. In the Roman Catholic Church I found that stability that I sought.

On the one hand there was her teaching regarding the Second Coming, which I myself felt, on intuitive grounds, to be imminent; there was her teaching on the Final Judgement, which satisfied completely my thirst for *seeing* justice done, for I was told that this judgement would be one of nations as well as individuals; would be public and inescapable. Above all did the Roman Catholic Church alone teach a doctrine that was coherent and meaningful to me, on the true greatness of the mother of Christ, her role in the scheme of salvation, her position as Queen of Heaven. Both my own beloved prophets – G. K. Chesterton and Hilaire Belloc – were Roman Catholics, and I started to read them afresh and right through. I found them very very good.

Concurrently with these apocalyptical-type doctrines was set

the 'strict moral code'. It was clear that here was an aspect of
Roman Catholic teaching that I would have to master if I
were ever to reach the stature of a 'proper' Roman Catholic,
rather than the kind of uncommitted hanger-on that I otherwise
felt myself to be.

With a sense of dedication I proceeded along the path which
led eventually to my being received into the Church. Once in,
I determined that with the help of Almighty God I would be
as well informed and devout a Roman Catholic as possible.
That precept, once determined, became my guiding light; one
that I have tried to follow, and always will.

Soon after this I met my first real Pole, and was very pleased
when he asked me to marry him. I found no difficulty in
agreeing. The plight of the Polish regular army officers, left
high and dry at the end of the war, unable to return home,
unfitted for civilian life, is well known to all, and requires no
elaboration from me. They were penniless, uprooted, exiled,
disorientated, and lost. I was glad to make this condition my
own, not for the sake of any of these things in themselves, but
rather for the sake of my beloved who *was* these things.

And that is how it all began. I was now 21 years old. I had
acquired a vision, a faith, and the status of matrimony, in
that order.

I was also busy acquiring a formal education, and had indeed
achieved my B.Sc. at nineteen, and was now proceeding
through the medical curriculum. Looking back I must say I
am astonished at the mildness of the Dean of my Faculty, who
contented himself with the observation that I did not seem to
have my entire mind on my work!

CHAPTER III

THE CRISIS

ONE could say that the first seven years of my married life were productive. I was still learning to live and be a conscientious Roman Catholic, to be a good wife, to acquire further degrees and medical qualifications; digest the hurly burly of basic hospital training; finding jobs and – perhaps more important – keeping them. In this time we moved house five times. Nor was I neglectful of my other duties, in the eyes of the Church, for I was delivered of four babies. I would say a not uneventful period in my life.

By the middle of 1955 I held the post of Registrar at a large mental hospital in the north of England.

Suspicion dawned that a domestic crisis was approaching. Our house went with my job. I could see for myself and quite clearly that I could not continue to hold this, or any other job, if I continued to give birth to children with such regularity. Neither was it easy for my husband. The language itself presented a formidable hurdle for him. As a qualified lawyer and Judge Advocate in his own country, there were no reciprocal qualification arrangements for his profession in this country. He had to struggle hard for his livelihood, heavily handicapped by his own sense of personal pride. This pride, naturally enough, barred him from renouncing his Polish nationality; and thus precluded from British citizenship, neither was he eligible for a grant to requalify in this country. So did we serve our allies.

We had problems, both of us. I sought relief in my religion and my husband in introspection and reinforcement of sturdy, if stubborn, Polish independence.

As most married folk should easily realise, problems like ours can either break a marriage or throw the couple closer together. And the closer we got, the very communion of matrimony, that which binds and comforts a couple in adversity could only lead to yet another baby. . . .

Truly a cruel dilemma, so I set about to arm myself to meet the inevitable crisis.

Every influence in my life was combining to assure me that the time had come to limit my family, and consolidate my professional status. I became aware, with great alarm, that if I allowed myself to be moulded by these influences I would lose my hold on my vision, which was now incorporated into my own image of myself. My vision and my faith were now one, and if I lost my hold on one I would lose the other, and suffer disintegration of personality.

I explained the danger I felt I was in to the Roman Catholic chaplain at the hospital where I worked, and he seemed to understand for he had doubtless come across problems like this before. He advised that I should procure the services of an able spiritual director, and he then recommended one to me by name. He also explained to me that for spiritual direction to work in accordance with the whole Roman Catholic spiritual theory one must place oneself in a position of total submission to the advice of the director, and orientate oneself to this opinion as though it were our Lord in person giving it. It is the duty of the one directed to give the director all the information he might be reasonably supposed to need in order to come to a responsible decision. The director may be argued with and sworn at, but in the end he must be obeyed. If this is not understood at the outset, one is strongly advised not to embark. One is also warned, in all fairness, that the game is a dangerous one from many points of view. At the same time it should be born in mind that all serious Roman Catholic spiritual authorities make it quite clear that without such voluntary and total subjection to the will of another no real spiritual progress can be made.

Help was a necessity if I was to preserve my marriage, my husband's love, my faith, my job, everything.

The director I was advised to approach was known as a kind and able priest, generous with his time and understanding. He agreed to 'take me on'.

I explained to him the nature of my dilemma: how the demands of domestic life were threatening my chances of professional advancement. I explained how my particular speciality, psychiatry, was an exceptionally demanding one as far as emotional resources go, and how thin these resources were wearing. I explained that my husband was all but submerged by his own inescapable difficulties. I sought his approval to the idea of me, then and there, handing in my resignation, and devoting myself entirely to my task of being a competent wife and mother. It was necessary to seek the approval of another for such a step, for it would leave the family homeless, and as we were without capital it would mean 'trusting in Providence' to find us a home. My relations had already remarked, with considerable justice – though in another context altogether – that 'trust in Providence' was a fancy Roman Catholic name for the simple expedient of getting someone else to hold the baby.

My director seemed to take a similar view, or rather gave it as his considered opinion, that there was no justification for taking Providence by storm. Providence was, then and there, supplying the family with approximately £1,000 a year, and a home, through my job; and he considered it my plain duty to hang on to these benefits as long as possible.

This judgement I accepted, though in the course of the next eighteen months, as total physical and emotional collapse assailed me (I had my fifth child and a miscarriage in this period), I repeatedly queried it. On each occasion I received the same answer: I was not free to abandon my profession.

I was accused at the time, by colleagues and relations, of acting irresponsibly in thus allowing myself to reach such a dangerous point of exhaustion. My defence to them was: 'I was acting under obedience.' I see now of course that this is no defence. The responsibility for putting myself under a director was mine. If my director considered any of the responsibility his, he has certainly kept marvellously quiet about it, and has done so to this day.

In view of the current and increasingly fashionable teaching by Roman Catholic authorities about sexual abstinence as the remedy for such a dilemma as mine, it seems to me astonishing that my director never put this to me as a solution, backing up such advice by personal contact with my husband and insistence on his co-operation. His advice was of the old fashioned kind that insists that a wife should never refuse her husband love. In this he was facing realistically the difficulties of my own situation but totally failing to take into account the intolerable physical strain that this line of conduct places upon the wife, especially the wife who is contributing more than half the total family income.

There is a duality in Roman Catholic teaching at the moment, between which the devout wife cannot help but fall. When her marriage is in danger she is taught about the beauty of sacrificial love. When her life is in danger she is taught the necessity of 'self control'.

The simple truth was that I was being slowly crushed to death by my director's too rigid interpretation of Catholic doctrine. And this crushing and this dying was taking place in full public view, yet neither he nor any single member of my Church seemed to consider it his business.

We were a Christian family in need and we needed a solution that could be given with the full authority of the Roman Catholic Church. If it were the inflexible will of God that my marriage should be cemented by the sacrificial love that my director was demanding of me, then was it not that same director's business to see that the Church, for which he claimed to speak, came to my aid in the matter of helping with such matters as domestic help, and even further with finance, when our own home and the income I was contributing were lost, by my incapacitation through child-bearing?

Even then I suspected that my (our) problem was not an isolated one. Indeed some of the inmates of the very mental hospital in which I was working were living testimonies of the havoc this problem could play on the human mind.

But in all this I am anticipating. . . . At this time my director had me nailed firmly to the dual role of wife and doctor, and to help me fulfil my obligations in these fields he gave me the following principles to work on.

1. *My husband I must always try to put first in my thoughts and feelings, and on no account must I ever refuse him love.*

When I pointed out the danger to my health and competence in my job, if these embraces should lead to another pregnancy, he replied that that danger was entirely subordinate to my duty to love my husband, *and as long as I did that, God would look after me.*

2. *As regards my professional work, he gave me as a formula to work on:* 'see Christ in mental patients'.

When I pointed out that to do so in earnest would involve giving far more time and attention and sympathy to my patients than was common practice in my hospital, his answer was *that it was my Christian duty to do so, and God would look after me.*

So now I must get busy on this second, but at least remotely possible, edict.

A shadowy figure of the 'good doctor' already lived in the back of my mind, a composite figure made up of childhood recollections of the family doctor, schoolday lessons of the historical figures of early medicine, more recent remembrances of University professors and some of those 'statesmen' of medicine with whom I had had contact since qualifying and practising in my own right.

Was this what my spiritual director wanted of me? Shades of Hippocrates with maybe a touch of the patience and courage of Johan Weyer (the sixteenth-century Dutch physician who had been the first medical man to make an effective stand against the witch hunters of his day). Or was it perhaps the penetration and wholly admirable perseverance of Freud?

Yes, Freud: that is who he would have in mind. Here was a physician of heroic stature; here was one who would never forsake a patient. He would learn from his patients but never forsake them. . . . Was there here a critical note creeping in? Could I have been thinking about what the Church has been known to do time and time again when failing to understand one of her children? The custom of pronouncing anathemas? The anathematised were here and now, before my eyes, coming under the care of psychiatrists.

There is some truth here, for it is indeed certain that psychiatry is medicine's general dumping ground. People come along into mental hospital and are examined according to accepted custom and placed in this or that diagnostic category and given this or that form of treatment and indeed it is wonderful how many recover and go home. There are, however, a certain embarrassing residue who can be placed in no diagnostic category. Their illness cannot be named, and treatment is a problem. The tendency is, or was in my day (7–10 years ago) to 'bang them on the head' and hope for the best. It is certain that a number of these so treated do recover, but there are always the ones who don't. These tend rather to get steadily worse, and the more so the more 'treatment' they receive. The failures of modern psychiatry are not boasted about, indeed they are not heard of at all. They are fed and clothed and nursed with kindness and kept decently out of sight.

I often thought that if only we had the orientation of Freud, who never attempted to impose anything on his patients, but rather placed himself passively before them in order to learn the truth from them, if our approach were to be of this nature and we had all the time and patience necessary to implement it, then *all* of these 'failures' could yet be cured. But we lacked these things and the failures lived on to haunt us.

Surely there was a place here for a doctor who could live and work my spiritual director's second instruction? I had been instructed to seek Christ in mental patients; so I sought Him, and pre-eminently, in patients such as these.

The idea had crossed my mind, that if Christ's Second Advent were to take the same stealthy and natural course as His first, and if we had indeed reached the time of His coming, then would He not impinge on society as an odd fellow who made a lot of crazy claims for himself? For this He would make himself no more popular with His relations and His neighbours than He did during His first coming. In those days it wasn't very easy to catch Him and shut him up, but in the end it was achieved and under adequate legal cover. Nowadays it would in a way be easier. If it can be shown by your neighbours that you constitute a serious menace to their peace of mind, and if they are sufficiently determined to silence you, it can be done. The victim's 'illness' is described to him in terms of his inability to adapt to society.

Many are the prophets, poets and artists who must have experienced this danger at some time. The more they are rejected by society, the more abnormal they become. There comes to be a sort of no-man's land between them and society, in which the wanderer is liable to become a sniper's target. When things get to this pass, it is often difficult to say who is primarily at fault, society or the misfit. If your prophet, struggling with his 'visitation', his prophecy, finds himself at odds with society, his danger is very real, and that is just as true in our free society as in a dictatorship; indeed it is worse in our society, for in a dictatorship he is officially considered 'bad', and he has to console him the long and illustrious line of predecessors who have suffered in the same cause, he also retains the sympathy and respect of the free world. In our society, however, once he has fallen foul of it, he is considered 'ill', and this adds to the burden of prophecy, that he is already carrying alone, and isolates him still further, and can indeed precipitate true insanity.

The very danger of this happening can induce a kind of panic in the doctor. The power of modern psychiatry, with its physical methods of treatment, including brain surgery, is very great indeed. Your prophet is in real danger of being literally destroyed.

If, however, he has the good fortune to meet a doctor who has real compassion and insight, he can be very greatly helped. He must indeed be convinced that John the Baptist was not a man who *could* be lived with. Society tears and rends its prophets. Society suffers irreparable loss.

The prophet requires to appreciate that his message must be for society's good, and therefore, both for society's sake and his own, he must learn to integrate his message with his personality, and adapt both to the prevailing circumstances. If he fails to do this he will certainly lose his head, as his most illustrious predecessor John the Baptist (than whom the least in the Kingdom of Heaven is greater).

I began to see the task of psychiatry in these terms, in relation to my hypothetical Christ, hidden in my very real, 'Baptist-type' patients.

A psychiatrist can do little – as a psychiatrist – to influence society not to reject its prophets, but he *can* help the prophet so rejected to accept society as it is. If he is to be successful in this work he must show absolute respect for the content of his patient's mind. This is the prophetic material. The psychiatrist's task is to help him integrate this content with the natural man so that neither the man nor the message suffers loss.

I would remind my readers of the words of the prophet Joel: 'I will pour out my Spirit upon all mankind, and your sons and daughters will be prophets. Your old men shall dream dreams, and your young men shall see visions, everywhere servants and handmaids of mine inspired to prophecy! . . .

before the day of the Lord comes, the great and terrible day.'
(Joel 2: 28.)

I am aware that for many of my readers what I have written
in the last few pages will be incomprehensible. But for some it
will contain much meaning and it is for them that I write.
There is no reason why, just for this once, the world should not
wait while the needs of the prophets are attended to!*

With ideas such as these concerning the role of psychiatry
in the modern world beginning to take shape in my mind, I
left the practice of psychiatry behind me seven years ago.
During the time of their formulation I could only hope that
in my concurrent obedience to my spiritual director's first
edict, God (Providence, fate, hormones, luck or anything rather
than contraceptive devices) would keep me unpregnant long
enough to put them into practice.

It was not to be. My fifth pregnancy, and second miscarriage
following hard after, completed the rout of this 'good doctor'
from the contemporary psychiatric scene. I had had faith and
had submitted to my husband as directed to do and, as my
training had quite correctly led me to suspect, the resultant
pregnancies left me unfitted for any further medical work.

In leaving psychiatry, I left behind me the whole profession
of medicine, and I left with the solemn conviction that I would
never practice again.

My efforts to be a good wife and a good doctor had seemingly
failed, and the very effort of trying had robbed me of the ability
to be either. But for all that, the lessons were well worth
learning: I knew now some of my own limitations, and above
all I had learned *to put not my trust in man*.

* For much of this I am indebted to the work by Father Victor White,
O.P., *God and the Unconscious*.

CHAPTER IV

THE CONFLICT

So, in the end my parents *were* left holding the baby. Perhaps they were not altogether surprised. They had not been entirely with me when I had wanted to become a Catholic at the age of nineteen; indeed they had voiced their apprehension in no uncertain terms. Later, having spurned their advice on this matter, I did not even hear their objections to my marriage to a Pole. These objections I had laughed to scorn, trampled underfoot. Had I not 'the faith' itself, would they not live to see my Catholic faith and Polish husband vindicated in the sight of the whole world? 'If you doubt my ability to make good this boast,' I told them, 'it is because you doubt the power of the living God.'

Well, whatever anyone likes to say about that, they now certainly *had* me. They also had my five children, from ages seven downwards. This was the daughter whom they had sent to Aberdeen, twelve years previously from this same house to which she now returned. Her career in ruins, her health shattered, without money, without a foothold in the world, and *with five children*. This was the daughter that the Roman Catholic Church handed back to her parents.

What were they to do? They loved their daughter, they loved their grandchildren. The authority that they considered had brought her to this pass had, apparently, no suggestions to make, no help of any kind to offer. So they offered what they had, and that was a loving home. It was a home in which money was not over-plentiful, a home that entertained all shades of opinion and a strange diversity of views, the only criterion being that all beliefs must be honestly held, and the holders prepared to defend their views against all comers.

It was, of course, quite natural that my parents should feel deeply anxious about the possibility of further additions to the family. Though space and money were certainly problems, they were by no means the issues that primarily troubled their minds. They were honestly of the opinion that I could not stand the physical and mental strain of another pregnancy. And this fear was based, not only on the evidence before their eyes, but on solid and solemn medical opinion.

Within six months I conceived. My parents and doctors bowed their heads, and held their breath, hoping of course for the best. The best happened. A sixth beautiful baby was added to the family. I was apparently none the worse. Everyone breathed again. The baby was christened in style, but already and over these very celebrations was hanging the unspoken question: 'Do you suppose she will go and do it again?'

I was by no means happy. I needed a home of my own, my children to myself. The latest birth added greatly to the strain of trying to maintain a sense of family unity (by which I mean Bieżanek family unity). The whole strain of the situation became focused in that one burning question: how soon was there to be another baby?

For how long could my parents reasonably be supposed to endure this uncertainty? I myself had no answer to give them. In the home, wherein we were all squeezed, I was becoming conscious of what appeared to be nothing less than an organised conspiracy to rob me of my Catholic faith. As it was my faith alone that gave any meaning to my miseries, I must needs arm myself to defend this faith with my very life. Of course, in actual fact there was no conspiracy at all. There was simply an earnest discussion, amongst all the people most concerned regarding the means that might be legitimately employed to get me to see reason. Reason, I think, meant a simple admission on my part that until I had at least a home of my own, it would not be right for me to have another baby.

As can be imagined, the anxiety and tension created by this problem became very great indeed, situated as we were, so much on top of one another. Gradually it began to seem desirable to all concerned (except me) that I should be placed once again under the care of a good psychiatrist. When it did come to the push, I could not resist. I was physically very overtired with the new baby (a night-screamer, as it happened), distraught with the implications of the trap I could see closing in on me, and harassed beyond words by the failure of all con-

cerned to see that, above all things, the solution lay in helping
us get our own home.

In fairness to my parents on this point, it must be remembered
that in my conduct to date, in regard to my child-bearing
activities, they had no reason to suppose that I was not, indeed,
infected with a virus of insanity. They, after all, had never
followed the arguments put up by the Church on this matter.
They had not heard my spiritual director holding forth, in
such powerful terms, about the beauty of leaving aside all for
the love of Christ. How great an honour it was for a woman to
die in this cause, the very same cause for which all the Catholic
martyrs had died, the cause of Holy purity, without which there
is, nor can be, anything holy. No, they had never heard words
like this, repeated day in and day out. When I tried to remedy
this educational deficiency, can they be altogether blamed for
concluding that I was, indeed, a little touched?

But it is necessary to understand that the danger that they
most feared was not – repeat *not* – my death. For by this time
we were all so wrought up that I doubt if any of us cared *who*
lived or died. It was the danger to the future of their six
grandchildren. This was the problem that tormented them. If I
was incapacitated, due to whatever cause, who, they asked,
was to care for the children? Approaching their sixties as they
then were, and still with a child of their own to finance through
University, how *could* they let me suppose that my formula:
'Providence will provide' was sufficient to meet the actual needs
of the situation? Had I not indeed maintained the very same
in the past? And *what* had Providence provided? It had provided
them with a large problem family firmly entrenched in their
house. What did I suppose Providence had up its sleeve this
time, if I did indeed achieve my apparent aim of dying for my
faith? 'You are not *free* to die,' they stormed at me. Ah now,
that is the whole point, was I or wasn't I?

It was indeed with no little relief that I escaped into the
quiet of an Edinburgh mental hospital. There for five weeks
I slept, ate, swallowed the pills I was given, argued with my
doctors and thought.

The question my doctors put to me was: 'How do you suppose
we can regard you as anything less than a plain menace to
society? Why should the needs of your soul, as you understand

them, be allowed to disrupt the entire lives of your whole family?'

I began to think with envy of those of my fellow inmates who had long since given up the struggle and lived in that hospital as in a true asylum from the world.

I thought myself round and round, but a solution evaded me. I became stronger in mind and body, but answer I had none to give.

My problem was this, how could my own marriage survive without the bond of sexual union that my husband demanded? My psychiatrists were assuring me that it could not. How could I survive in my parents' home if more babies were to come? I knew I could not.

What was I to do?

At this point I began to suppose, with an agonised dismay, that I must be the only Catholic with a problem of an order as great as this.

The all but total failure of my 'intellectual' Catholic friends and relations, including my erstwhile spiritual director, to compassionate me in my agony, to be pierced by it, or even to acknowledge its existence, was the worst part of the suffering that I then endured. I was standing out for what I had been taught to believe was a fundamental Catholic doctrine and hardly a Catholic I knew seemed interested.

If these words should strike the non-Catholic as nothing better than a wail of self pity, betraying a kind of welfare state mentality, as though I were saying 'Why should I help me, its somebody else's job to worry for me', then I will say now that until the reasoning that underlay my complaint is understood the reason for the bitterness that is about to tear the whole Roman Catholic body will not be understood.

We Roman Catholics believe that we are all cells of the one Body, the Body of Christ, whose head is Christ Himself. When one member dies (through sin) the whole body suffers loss. To sever oneself from this body by any act of one's own will is not only to incur eternal death, but to damage the body as a whole. A member of this body, finding himself forced by influences outside the Church to commit this act of spiritual outrage, might reasonably expect succour from the body as a whole.

In my case, and as I have discovered since, in the case of a multitude of others (who do not write books about themselves), such an interest has not been forthcoming.

For this reason did I, in these bleak days, begin to see my personal dilemma as one that was bringing judgement day itself to the intellectuals of my Church.

Six months later I conceived again. And that I suppose was my answer, my answer *then*. I knew that what I needed above all things was my own home. This problem could not be really faced, let alone solved, until I established my own centre of gravity. The answer when it came must come from inside me, it could not be imposed from without. It was my problem, my very own. I must needs take it to my bosom and nurse it. For indeed, if it came to pass that the solution I found was to cost me my life – and I had strong premonitions that it would – then let me at least lay down my life of my own free will. Let no one ever say that any man had taken it from me.

Thus it was that our seventh child was conceived. And thus did my parents' agony reach a new depth. And thus did we leave their home. During the next six weeks the turmoil and uncertainty reached their climax.

A Roman Catholic family in Wallasey showed great hospitality in taking us in, but our plight was indeed desperate. We had six children scattered, a seventh on the way. We had no home and no money with which to buy one.

What we actually needed was a loan of £200 for a period of three years, for in that time that amount of money was coming to us. We understood that £200 would secure a deposit on a house. To raise £200 there and then was the problem. During these six weeks I wrote over thirty letters to Catholic relations, to medical societies, to priests and bishops who were known to me and who were already acquainted with our problem. I wrote and begged for the mercy of this loan. I received the same number of replies that all said the same thing: there was no money available.*

In these days did I begin to learn the meaning of despair.

Non-Catholic friends and relations were quite frankly indis-

---

* I believe that now there is a Catholic housing society, being formed in some dioceses, whose aim is to give this kind of financial assistance to Catholic families in this kind of need, but four-and-a-half years ago on Merseyside there was no such thing.

posed to help as they did not approve of the course my marriage had taken, and wanted to have no part in appearing to encourage either me or my husband in thinking that we were an 'investable' proposition.

This view is one that I can understand. I cannot to this day understand the mentality of the 'good' of my own Church, who could so lightly dismiss the social problem we presented as simply none of their business.

But through the intervention of a most merciful Providence a solution came to us. We met again the same priest who still was the chaplain at the same mental hospital where I had once worked. As in the past he had shown an understanding of my problem, so did he now. By his quiet confidence in God's goodness, he banished all despair and set us at once praying a nine-day prayer to Blessed Martin de Porres, in whom he himself had great faith. He backed up this piety with the most realistic offer to date – a pledging of himself as guarantor for our mortgage payments.

Within the nine-day period, which by some strange chance ended on the feast day of St. Stanislaus, the patron saint of Poland, we became the owners of our first real home. Two Roman Catholic women friends in Scotland, hearing of our plight, had stepped in and simply sent the necessary money for the deposit. I had originally hesitated to ask these people, because I had already experienced their boundless goodness, and felt strongly that this was a truly social problem and one that I wished some authority in my Church to recognise as such. But this was not to be. These two friends solved it, with the silence, the swiftness and the competence of love itself.

Thus was the family gathered into one. And thus did we move with great confidence and joy into our own real home, our first. And here in this home, soon after, was our seventh child born. And here we are to this day.

Deo gratias.

CHAPTER V

THE RESOLUTION

So at last we had our own home. Never again could we say 'if only we had a house of our own. . . .' For now we had it, and with it the chance to build that true and lasting marital relationship that had always seemed so difficult when all our actions had had, perforce, to come under the scrutiny and criticism of others upon whom we had been dependent.

Above all did I now feel that I could vindicate my faith and prove to all that it could work and was therefore true. In my mind's eye I could see myself giving birth to many more children. I saw then, 'the laying down of life' in terms of turning my back on all worldly considerations and making the idea of the large Catholic family work. I knew that, in a sense, whatever I could prove by what I achieved would have a Universal validity. My husband received a working man's pay. We had no other source of income. He looked forward to no pension, neither of us possessed a life insurance. So we were poor, not very poor, but poor in a straightforward sort of way, like most people.

I had no desire to get back to my profession. I only wanted to be the good Catholic mother, presiding over a large and happy family, and now that all outside interference was removed, I had not the slightest doubt of my ability to achieve this.

The first thing I noticed as being wrong was the fact, the inescapable fact, that I simply had too much to do. With the birth of my new baby I now had four children under five years to attend to. The sixth child was still a night-screamer. These two youngest children alone, for over a year, had me out of bed three or four times a night, every night. I was isolated in my house, and without friends. My husband was hardly ever at home. Every decision fell upon me to make. All the anxieties of illness and what-have-you were my exclusive concern. Being over-tired, I was constantly irritable with the children. We had no television. Any sort of family entertainment I had to supply from inside my own head. Tied with the children, I never went out. I never met anyone. Reading is not easy in a house full of children. I found my mind simply seizing up on me. In other words, it did not take me long to find my promised land not entirely to my liking. Actually, it was worse than this. In my constant battle to stop the chores getting on top of me, I was becoming coarsened, mentally and physically. Not – please note – refined by labour and suffering, in the manner that so many spiritual books would lead one to suppose, but simply coarsened. I wanted, above all things, not to have children getting under my feet, not always to have two or three shouting simultaneously to gain my attention. I wanted to be relieved from those torments more than I wanted anything else. Let them get out of the house away from under my feet. I didn't care sometimes where they went or what they did, provided they left me enough elbow room in which to prepare the next meal. These, of course, are no original observations, but experiences common to all mothers of large families. I had constantly and frequently, as a doctor, heard others complaining of just these things. It was only now that I was experiencing their full and undiluted horror for myself.

The second thing wrong with my 'promised land' was an insufficiency of money. My husband's earnings in the British merchant navy were sufficient to support the nine of us as long as half the family were toddling and the older children attending only primary school. As soon as the eldest started at grammar school, the squeeze began in earnest. Uniform, bus fares, subscriptions for this and that, pocket money, all items perhaps not great in themselves, but taken all together, and multiplied by two as the second child passed his eleven plus, all amounted to a problem in itself a waking nightmare.

The anxious faces of the children as they hesitatingly told me of the money they had to have for this and that were a continual reproach. My explosions of irritability and wrath at every mention of these modest and innocent requirements precluded any possibility of true family happiness.

The notion of 'holy poverty' was one that had appealed to me from early days. What I had failed to take into account was the fact that modern society simply will not allow her members to be 'poor' in that sense. Children have to stay at school until at least 15 years old, they have to wear shoes and socks, they have to wear the uniform of the school the state assigns them to. They have to look properly fed. To our grandparents these things might have sounded like the very height of luxurious living, but to us here and now they are examples of the kind of basic minimum we must supply our children with if we are to escape prosecution for neglect. Will childless ecclesiastics please take note?

Against this background, the thought of another pregnancy, with the nausea and tiredness it brings in its own right, took on the prospect of a nightmare. Just the thought of it. I was not then rejecting the idea of ever having more children. It was pregnancy itself, then and there, that could not be permitted.

Thus did my husband's brief and unpredictable appearances in the home become in themselves a source of torment. As I wished the children out of my way, so did I wish him. When his presence was added to my broken nights and chronic sleeplessness, I used to feel, and say, that if he as much as touched me I would take a running jump at the window.

Sex, being inextricably linked in my mind with child-bearing, now became my obsession. Help was to be had from no one. Even sympathy I could hardly expect. When sought for from Catholic friends and relations, I would be speedily and unfailingly reminded that I now had all that I had ever asked for. Thus was I driven down the suddenly fashionable, Roman Catholic line of thought that maintained that the solution to all marital problems of my type lay in the abolition of sex. My husband had to be banished from my presence, into a room of his own. Everything in me that attracted him to me and me to him had to be suppressed. All this I attempted, and heaven is my witness.

With what result? My home, my heaven on earth, the land of my dreams, was taking on the characteristics of Belsen. Hate had become the order of the day. In such an atmosphere, even prayer, or shall we rather say, above all things, prayer, becomes the most dangerous activity. When you pray, you must needs let your defences down, you must lay yourself open to the influence of a loving and generous Spirit. The next thing would be that you find yourself betrayed into actually kissing your husband good-night, and from then on. . . .

So I had come home to Belsen after all. The very place from which I had started out on my journey to avoid. I had made a full circle and faced Nothing.

I told my parents that I felt I must now start using contraceptives and that they ought to be the first people to know. Their explosion of relief and joy is only to be matched by the intensity of their affection for each and every one of their grandchildren.

But I, as I swallowed my pills, was sad. I knew myself to be presiding over the burial of a great and grand and noble idea. An idea to which I had come to identify myself so closely, that in a sense I was burying myself.

Who, I wondered, would lay flowers on my tomb?

Flowers, that reminded me of something. Did not Keats in his dying feel flowers growing over him? If Keats could give utterance to a thought so strange, in words that were destined to pierce the very souls of poets yet unborn, could not I?

I was dying . . . but could not my very death be given a shape that could take on meaning for others? Had I not promised myself that no man would take my life, but rather would I lay it down of my own free will? Did I not *feel* the roots of a new era of thought groping and growing in the darkness that was my soul?

To revert to Belloc's ballad. I could now say indeed:

'Steep are the seas and savaging and cold,
    in dark waters terrible to try'

Could I add with the same confidence:

'But thou shalt lead me to the lights,
    and I shall hymn thee in a harbour story told. . . .'?

CHAPTER VI

HOW THE CLINIC OF
SAINT MARTIN DE PORRES
CAME INTO BEING

Now I had taken the plunge. Swallowing my very first tablet of my first month's supply was a moment of the greatest possible significance. . . . I knew I was entering into a new kind of life. But, again, I anticipate.

First I had to obtain the pill and this entailed a consultation with my family physician. How could he have realised what a great step I was proposing to take? Poor man, he could not. He was not a Roman Catholic and could have had no notion of the extent of the opposition of the clergy to this latest medical aid. Here I am not referring only to 'opposition' in the sense of the written word, but of that far more powerful and telling condemnation that takes place in the secrecy of the confessional, in which the most formidable spiritual sanctions are both threatened and applied.

It seemed to me important that my family doctor should understand the theological and moral implications. He told me that I was hardly the first Roman Catholic woman to consult him on this subject, and he must have been surprised at the extent of the fuss I was making. But I wanted him to understand, I wanted everyone to understand, and I still do. . . .

What was I to do with all that vast store of spiritual energy that had, up to this point, been concentrated into keeping faith with the Church's doctrines on this one issue?

I had conceived all these children in the faith, the faith that assured me that if I did what the Church taught God would look after me, but if I once started to disobey, then nothing (except speedy repentance) could save me from the torture of everlasting fire.

At this point the Church, in the person of one of the assistant priests in the parish, was kind enough to call. This I might say was the first parochial visitation since we had come to the parish two years previously, apart that is from one very brief call soon after arrival. (All the time that I had been struggling alone with all the fiends of hell, no one called, though I had let them know that I was in great need. A doctor who ran his practice thus would very soon have no patients left.)

Anyway, with this priest I went over the ground and showed him the bottle of contraceptive pills that the doctor had prescribed. I asked him if he had any other alternative line of conduct to suggest.

He said he had not.

I asked him if he would help me separate from my husband, as if I *was* being driven into hell fire it would seem to be my husband's failure to keep the Church's rules rather than mine that would be responsible.

He said he could not so help. So I asked him if in view of these considerations he would not agree to give me the sacraments of confession and communion.

He said he could not consider doing such a thing.

I asked him if he would refer the matter to the parish priest with a view to referring it to the Bishop.

He said, 'That would be a waste of time.'

I said, 'What then am I to do?'

He answered '*I do not know.*'

So I started in and swallowed my pills on the prescribed date – May 25th, 1962 – and waited for the world to come to an end.

The world did not oblige.

I came away on holiday to Cornwall with the children, and all the time I was blazing away in mind and talking and talking to every one who would listen. 'I have been turned out of my own church,' I wailed, 'for doing no more than what my doctors have obliged me to do, what my husband wants me to do – and what have I done? I have simply tried to save my home. . . . Is there any sorrow like unto my sorrow?' The people who received this barrage of complaint all listened in polite silence, then admitted that they knew not what to say to comfort me. They themselves, being Christians of other denominations, did not have this problem. They themselves practised contraception and their religion without difficulty or fear. Nor did they appear to be disintegrating in their moral lives as a result. Far from it. But apart from suggesting that I leave the Church that was causing me so much heartbreak, they could find nothing else to say.

What could my answer be to that? Was not my whole concept of the life of Christ in my soul dependent upon the Roman Catholic Church? It was the Roman Catholic Church that had made me what I was, for she alone had been the guiding light of my life. Now she was telling me that I had reduced myself to the level of a prostitute, by seeking to supply a means for male gratification in return for money. That the man in question is your husband does not affect the validity of this argument. For marriage, being a sacrament for Catholics, is bound up with the presence of divine grace in the soul. By my 'mortal sin' in taking these pills, I had destroyed that life of grace, my whole sacramental life was destroyed, and therefore everything in my marriage that served to make it holy and different from the union of animals. Indeed it is worse because animals are innocent, but I was guilty of a *monstrous sin that made my soul hideous* and brought me down to a level with the very lowest moral lepers.

This realisation released in me a flood of compassion for prostitutes themselves. If I, the 'holy and the pure', could find myself over-night precipitated into their ranks, as it were, by factors quite beyond my control, then what unspeakable injustices of male pride and arrogance lay behind the path trodden by such women? The text spoken to the Pharisees: 'I tell you that the publicans and the harlots will enter the kingdom of heaven before you', was a source of some consolation. But it did not supply an answer to the question: 'How am I to bring up my children?' Up to this point I had been teaching them with great fervour the necessity of practising their religion with regularity and precision and to this end had set them the best example I could, but now I had no example to set them. How could I go to Mass and worship our Lord in the Blessed Sacrament, if by my perfidy I had so offended that same Christ that He could find no place in my soul? But if I did not go to Mass, why should my children go? If I urged them, would they not sense hypocrisy, and begin to detest, to distrust, the very religion they were sent to church to participate in? But where else were they to go to learn the words that taught everlasting life?

Should I take them from their Catholic schools and send them to other schools and to churches of another denomination? But how would I explain the sudden change to them? And even if I could explain it, would my Catholic husband agree? Indeed he would not! If I were to attempt any such thing the domestic strife that I had set out to cure by my 'sin' would be visited on my head ten times over. No, the muddle and the cruelty of the priests and the parents ought not to be visited on the children, rather let the children make their own way in the Catholic faith, in which path I had already set them, and surely God would keep them.

So it came to be November, 1962, and on December 8th would be the anniversary of my eldest daughter's first Holy Communion. 'You never go to Communion now Mummy, in fact you don't go to Church at all, please come with me and receive Communion on December 8th.' In this she was being a good Catholic and repeating the lesson she had learned at school, a lesson inculcated by nuns who were good women and doing no more than their simple duty in exhorting their charges to encourage their parents to greater fervour. 'Yes dear, I probably will,' I said to her, and a look of great trouble lifted from her face.

Then, possessed as it were, I called upon the same assistant priest who had visited me previously, and told him that I was still on the pill, that my health had improved beyond recognition and that marital relations had improved to the point where I felt my home to be no longer in jeopardy, and in view of these blessings and the danger to my children's faith, if I continued to stay away from Church, would he reconsider the question of my being allowed to receive Communion?

His answer was that there was nothing to reconsider.

I said, 'Well, if I come up to the altar rails, will you pass me over?'

His answer was that he probably would, because he could not give it me.

I said that as far as I could see, his approach was entirely negative.

I was struggling with a problem too big for me and, seeing

that the clergy are supported by the laity, it would seem only just that they interested themselves in their people's problems.

'Have you yet done as little as speak to the parish priest? No? Well, from now on I am going to make it my business to see that you do *something*, even if it's only having to make a point of not giving me Communion. I will be coming to the altar rails with my daughter on the 8th of December and what you choose to do about it is your business.' And I added that he now had just two weeks left in which to consult his superiors and decide upon a course of action.

At the same time I put the matter in writing and sent it to the parish priest.

I received no answer to this letter, and so on the morning of December 8th, 1962, I went to St. Alban's, Wallasey, to the Mass I said I would be going to, 7.30 a.m., with my daughter, and went up with her to the altar rails.

I was given Communion by the same priest, Father James Gaskell, who had said he would not give it to me.

Whether this reflected a personal decision of his own, or was the result of an 'instruction' I do not know. But then and there I took it as a sign from heaven, a sign that said in God's eyes I *was* acceptable.

From then on I went to Church regularly and received Communion regularly.

My husband appeared relieved at this outcome, though remains to this day apparently unaware of the extent of the spiritual turmoil that had led to it. His view is that it is a woman's duty to practise her religion and to see that the children practise, and any associated difficulties are her exclusive concern.

Well, I continued in this manner, becoming increasingly sure of myself, until the end of February, 1963, when the Bishop came to the parish, and I made an appointment to see him. To him I explained what had happened – how it had come about that I was receiving Communion regularly and yet practising contraception in a manner condemned by the Church. I explained that a lot of people now knew this to be the case and I said that I could see that the position was serious and potentially very scandalous, and that I thought he ought to know. I said that if he needed time to look into my case, and was willing to do so, discuss it with his fellow bishops even, I would co-operate to the best of my ability, and refrain from embarrassing him and his clergy, for as long a time as he needed. I would stop going up for Communion and await his considered verdict.

He replied that there was nothing further to consider, that there was no question of a Church court of 'hearing', that the matter was plain, I was by my use of contraceptives transgressing an immutable law of God, and by continuing to receive our Lord I was guilty of sacrilege. I said that that was his view and I had another. However, in view of the extremely dangerous nature of my case, from his point of view, due to the fact that I was a doctor and was in a position to influence others, I would make one more suggestion.

I would voluntarily abstain from receiving Communion with no conditions, if he would explain to my children, *why* their mother could not receive. I would send them up to him and he could see them in private and explain in any terms he thought fit.

He said he could not do this, so I took my leave of him and continued as before, going to Church and receiving Communion every week.

Following on this interview with the Bishop, I became convinced that God wanted me to make this stand, and that it was He who had brought me so near to despair, so that I should learn for myself how bullied and wretched Catholic women are. It became my desire to help such women. Though my husband works hard and constantly, he is not able to earn enough to fully supply his large family with all its growing needs. So when my mind turned to what useful professional work I could take up, I thought at once of the Family Planning Association, with whom, up to this point, I had had no contact. I asked if I could take their training course, with a view to obtaining work in one of their clinics.

They accepted me for training and this in itself served as a blast of fresh air through my mind.

I met a different kind of woman with a different kind of outlook. Gradually did I begin to feel the 'battyness' with which I had been contending begin to subside. I became stronger and a more sensible and useful woman and doctor.

I was greatly impressed by the Family Planning Association, by its sanity and kindness, by its accessibility to all, by the welcome it extends to all and the consideration it shows to all.

I longed to bring some of these blessings into the Roman Catholic Church, where it seemed they were so urgently needed.

At the same time I wrote to Dr. Eleanor Mears, at the Family Planning Association's London headquarters, and told her that these were some of the good things I was thinking about her movement. In her reply, Dr. Mears asked if my letter could be published in the association's quarterly journal. I replied that indeed it could, but I would prefer it to appear anonymously. But of this letter later.

In the meantime I was disappointed to discover that there were no vacancies for doctors in any of the local Merseyside clinics. I was very keen to get started. Then the idea came to me, why not open a clinic of my own? No sooner thought of than done! The spare room was emptied of furniture, a wash basin installed and the necessary articles purchased. The very first item brought home was a statue of St. Martin de Porres. To him I dedicated my entire project.

St. Martin was, in his day, the kind of 'nigger' and the kind of 'doctor' of whom society did not think very highly. For all that, he contrived to do God's work in Peru in the sixteenth century, and the memory of his compassion has never failed. I felt that under the protection of one who was so despised and yet so successful, my little 'home-made' project could not fail.

At this stage I went to see my bishop again, at his home, and told him all about it. He listened to me very politely.

Through all this, my neighbours in Wallasey, mostly shop-keepers in adjacent streets to my home, were a great help to me. Their enthusiasm was marvellous. They seemed to seize upon the idea with gusto, they encouraged me greatly. They all seemed to realise that something important was afoot. I then went over to Liverpool and saw Archbishop Heenan and told him all about it. He also listened very politely.

On September 8th my clinic was opened. It happened that this date fell on a Sunday and the only celebrations were the ones in my own heart. September 8th is the day kept in our

Church as Our Lady's birthday, nine months exactly from the day of the commemoration of her conception, December 8th. It was on that day, nine months previously, that Father Gaskell had readmitted me to the Communion of my religion. On that day confidence had entered into my mind, and it might be said that on that day was my clinic conceived. And here it was, born on time.

Did this not mark the point of entry into the world of the Mother of God? The advent of this first full-scale birth control clinic in the world run by a Roman Catholic and a *practising* Roman Catholic at that? So tremendous did the implications of this event seem to me then that I was astonished at the absence of an 'extraordinary' sign, such as an earthquake. I did, however, later note with some satisfaction that my Bishop, who was then on pilgrimage to Lourdes, had on that day experienced a thunderstorm in the Pyrenees, of more than usual severity! With that I had to be content. Then I settled down to wait for patients.

At first, like any new practice, I wasn't exactly swamped with them. But thanks to the restoration of my self respect, my concurrent reintroduction into general practice assured me of an independent income, and therefore financial considerations of the clinic were non-existent.

There was no necessity for this private endeavour to be a business success. The rigid edict that applies to doctors, as it does to any professional person, forbids any form of advertising, and in any case advertising in any form would have been repugnant to me. That my clinic was open and available to give help was, in itself, sufficient. So, despite the initial paucity of patients, I had, as explained, abundant assurance that heaven itself was watching over the project, and having inspired the inception of this work could scarcely condone its dissolution.

I spoke to the parish priest about all this and tried to persuade him to give me absolution on all other counts and, if he could see his way, to suspending judgement on this particular matter. He refused, though he continued to give me Communion whenever I went up to receive.

So on I breezed. Then a friend who knew the Liverpool *Daily Mail* man asked if he could tell him my story. It was the end of November 1963 and the Council in Rome was winding up its second session and no word on the subject of birth control had been mentioned. It seemed to me that a public airing of the matter would do no harm and I agreed to meet the *Daily Mail*.

The following day there was a piece about a Wallasey woman doctor, a Roman Catholic, who was 'defying' her Church by running a birth control clinic. This headline was a source of some mortification for me, for I had made a long and exhaustive explanation concerning Roman Catholics' need for help and my belief that I had been 'called' to supply it. I had stressed that I had met with no opposition at all from any one in authority in the Church. To find such a 'Christian aid' programme described in terms of open rebellion was a little disconcerting. But there it was. A lot of time has been devoted since in conversations with fellow Catholics in which the correction of this initially 'defiant' impression has taken some doing. No matter, that *is* how the *Daily Mail* saw it and that is how they reported it. At my request, however, my name had not been given in the article.

Then it occurred to me that there might be other Roman Catholic women doctors in Wallasey who might be seriously embarrassed by leaving the question of identity so vague. I was pleased, therefore, when, on the same day Granada Television asked me over to Manchester to answer some questions on their programme 'Scene at 6.30'. I showed my face (anonymously) for just $1\frac{1}{2}$ minutes and answered questions that were simply confirmations of the *Daily Mail* story. That was on a Friday evening.

The following Sunday morning, December 1st, 1963, just thirty-six hours later, I went up for Communion as usual, with my children. The parish priest took the Communion plate from my daughter, who was before me, and passing in front of me, said out loud '*You don't get it*'.

This action of his was preceded by no warning or explanation from him. In fact it had been preceded by a twelve-month period in which I had been receiving Holy Communion regularly. During this time my views and actions and personal practice were known (I had made it my business to see they were known) to all concerned and had in no way altered (I had also made it my business to see that no doubt could be entertained on that matter either).

The only difference on this particular Sunday morning was that I had just done what I had always assured them I would do, and that was to 'shout the truth from the housetops'.

Unhappily the Bishop was still in Rome.

A few days later a priest from the parish called and said that I could not be readmitted to the sacraments until I had written to the Bishop and apologised. He declined to tell me on whose authority he brought this message. Having awaited the Bishop's return, I then wrote to His Lordship (the Bishop of Shrewsbury) and told him of the message I had been given and requesting his direction regarding the nature of the matter in which I had been deemed to offend him and the kind of apology that would be considered adequate.

The Bishop's reply stated that I was engaged in work running contrary to the direction of the Church's teaching, and as this work was attracting publicity, I was causing scandal and therefore could not be permitted to receive the sacraments until such a time as I would publicly renounce my present ways as erroneous.

I wonder what had been passing through his mind when I had talked to him first in the parish, nearly twelve months earlier, and again at his house in Shrewsbury, three months later? Did he suppose that I was some sort of a crank, destined for sure to come to grief and not really meaning a thing that I was saying? For this is certain: *never* once did he warn me that these would be the inevitable consequences that would overtake me should I continue in this my crusade. He certainly had not seen fit to take me up on my offer (made at our first meeting, and repeated several times in writing) to stay away from the sacraments altogether, until he had time to give the matter his full attention.

Did he suppose that I would not, in fact, have the strength to continue, and thus had allowed me to go on and on into a trap, the steel jaws of which had now closed behind me with such a sickening thud?

If any one thinks this action of my parish priest (that received this subsequent endorsement from our Bishop) was not serious for me, then they are mistaken. Not only did this sudden betrayal at the altar rails come as a great shock to myself, but was a source of harrowing distress and bewilderment to the children who were with me. As for my husband, though he was not with us in church, the effect of the public rebuff was equally electric, and indeed quite shattering.

Hitherto my husband had viewed my activities with a kind of benevolent interest. Suddenly it dawned on him that his wife had been branded a public sinner. Clearly it was not the activities themselves that worried him, it was the public branding, and as though taking his cue from the presiding priest, he proceeded to work his private vengeance.

He was bewildered and frightened and his vengeance had the cruelty that only bewilderment and fright can give.

I do not write this here to make out that I have suffered more from my husband than any Catholic wife might have done from any Catholic husband; rather do I write it to emphasise the truly desperate nature of the present muddle in the Roman Catholic Church. I have had women coming to my clinic showing me the bruises they have received from their husband's fists, as a result of trying to put into practice the Church's teaching on sexual abstinence. I have seen in mental hospitals the horrific end-products of a willingness on the part of wives to give in to their husband's demands for limitless sex without the protection of contraceptives. I have seen enough suffering on this question to know that my experience of it is but a 'type' and nothing more, and I present it here as nothing more. But these are facts that must be told. 'There is nothing done in the secret places that will not be shouted from the housetops.' Here and now is this prophecy being realised and I am honoured to know myself an instrument of its realisation.

In the meantime the letter that I had written six months earlier to the Family Planning Association was published in the January edition of their journal. In this, by an error, my name and address *were* disclosed. This was noted by the newspaper men who had been trying to establish the identity of the Wallasey woman doctor about whom the *Daily Mail* had written a month earlier. They appeared on my doorstep in droves and listened to my story with great interest and sympathy. I told the reporters that nothing so far had been said that could stop me from behaving as usual, going to Church regularly as was my custom, and also presenting myself at the altar rails for

Holy Communion whenever moved to do so. True, I had received a letter from the Bishop which could be construed as a sort of reprimand, a request (a royal request that brooked no argument) to discontinue my professional calling and to apologise to the public for having been so mistaken as to suppose that a Roman Catholic *could* ever come to conclusions at variance with the hierarchy. But I still felt that this was the Bishop's private view, and given in the way it was, did not in fact represent the considered verdict of the Most Holy Roman Catholic and Apostolic Church. Before this verdict can be given, the full facts of my case need to be known. I had no reason then to suppose that the Bishop did know them. Nor had he seemed unduly anxious to learn them. Remember, I had asked him for a full-scale, but private, Church enquiry into the facts of my case.

Such an enquiry I still await.

Since these days in January of this year (1964) I continued to go up for Communion in my own church with regularity, and was with equal regularity, 'passed over'. I have since received in other churches, in other dioceses, most notably in Westminster Cathedral on May 31st. This event was preceded by full and fair warning on my part that I would be coming with the intention of 'receiving'. I did in fact 'receive' and the whole event was given considerable press publicity.

Since the events of May 31st I feel free to participate in Holy Communion whenever and wherever I feel moved to do so and that without any longer going through the wearisome rigmarole of informing the clergy in charge of the exact time of my arrival, the mode of my dress, the colour of my hair. No priest could have been more fully informed of my intentions on May 31st than was the Archbishop of Westminster. He did not apparently feel the matter called for his personal attention.

On May 31st I received my freedom, not from Archbishop Heenan, whose conduct suggests that he does not greatly care what I do, but rather from the Queen of Heaven herself.

The feast of the Queenship of Our Lady is repeated every year on May 31st, and it can be prophesied with great assurance that with every year that passes will she show, with ever increasing power and authority, the extent of her sovereignty, both on Earth and in Heaven.

This is the 'sign' of May 31st, and it is one that I would ask all to take note of, be they scoffers or believers, Roman Catholic or otherwise.

> ... This is the faith that I have held and hold,
> and this is that in which I mean to die.

PART TWO

CHAPTER VII

THE WOMAN'S DILEMMA

IT is quite likely that woman's basic approach to sex is really no different from man's: the image of the beloved in the mind, the desire to pursue, to embrace, utterly to give the entire being, to *become*, as it were, the beloved.

This latent romanticism, common to both sexes, is perforce modified by the circumstances of a reality that is quite inescapable.

The most fundamental 'brake' upon the course of passion in the female is undoubtedly her own physical potentiality as mother. This biological fact has dominated and conditioned the female psyche since sentence was passed in the Garden of Eden. The terms of the sentence pronounced upon Eve were that henceforth was her husband to have dominion over her, that her conceptions were to be multiplied and in sorrow was she to bring forth children.

The long history of woman's sorrow in her position of bondage to man is in itself a most powerful testimony to the truth of Holy Scripture.

It is certain that physical dominance belongs to the male and it is equally certain that his sexual drive is more continuous than woman's.

The pleasures of the hunt and the chase culminating in the possession of the beloved in the final act of sexual union are those aspects of sexuality that man is free to make his own. Woman has not had this freedom, for that which is to the man simply 'the end of the affair' is to her but the beginning – very much so. Nor are the 'mere' inconveniences of pregnancy and parturition alone the simple end-product of a single coital act. Parturition itself is but the prelude to a new kind of existence, an existence dominated by a tiny bundle of humanity, that demands the total investment of herself.

The woman henceforth requires the continuous attention and

affection of the male in order to make life for herself, and her child, possible. To keep this attention she must needs (like it or not) offer more sex. More sex means more babies and she is now trapped indeed.

It is clear that the need for marriage is rooted deep in the human condition and that its permanence and stability are most essential for the woman.

It is equally clear that all the basic thinking regarding the 'laws' of marriage has been done by men.

In the development of a monogamous society men have sacrificed a great deal for the good of the female and this has perhaps left them slightly aggrieved. When only one partner is permitted to a man it must be irritating indeed to find that partner wearing herself out with childbearing, and wearing him out with complaints against a sexual drive that perhaps he knows not how to contain.

It must be very difficult for those whose only experience of marriage has been gained in a society where contraception and the possibility of divorce are taken as normal ingredients of marital life to appreciate how very different marriage appears to those who know none of these things. This different experience was common to all our forefathers and is still experienced by those of closely knit religious groups who do not admit the possibility of these 'aids to human happiness' as being ever lawful.

It is common for those of an older generation and of a stricter religious observance to point to a mounting divorce rate as evidence of a 'new' corruption, of an immorality that the older generation knew nothing about.

This author is of the strong suspicion that there is no truth in this supposition; present 'evidences of immorality' being merely a revelation of a state of affairs that has always prevailed but has hitherto been nicely walled up behind the respectable facade of 'Christian marriage'.

In the days when there was no possibility of escape, men and women simply tortured each other within their bedroom walls. The partner who got the worst of it was, undoubtedly, the woman.

The whole idea of a monogamous bond, raised by Mother Church to the status of an indissoluble sacrament, looks so impressive on paper. What could be neater or more satisfactory than the text-book definition of sacramental marriage? The contract freely entered into; the mutual giving and reception by the partners of rights over each other's bodies; the promise that this shall last until death; the assertion that this is God's doing and that a share in His life is offered to the partners who 'keep the rules'; that one of the rules is that there must be no man-made interference with the natural course of reproduction; that this is all God's doing and let no man intervene henceforth. . . . Why, it is marvellous! There we have the whole bag of tricks neatly tied up into one bundle. The whole problem of human sexuality solved by one simple formula, a formula that safely ensures the complete subjection of the female. Indeed, it has been marvellously done!

Before going into the question of why this is specifically unfair to the woman, it can first be said in general terms that the formula is certainly basically unfair to any Christian partner in the cases where the other partner shows himself or herself to be, in fact, not a Christian. It is not sufficient to say to the one who is loyally attempting to work the contract according to established Christian principles 'your partner's failure in the Christian life is your cross', for such a statement fails to take into account the fact of the existence of the family as a unity.

It is certain that a man and woman are free to embrace whatever private hell they choose, for the sake of their ideals, but it is by no means certain that they are free to inflict this hell on their children.

It is quite likely that there are as many divorces brought about by persons motivated by the highest Christian idealism who are seeking to save themselves and their children from the corrupting influence of a non-Christian spouse as there are brought about by simple promiscuity and resultant spite. It is also more than likely that many of these altruistically inspired divorces would have been unnecessary if an earlier and more realistic attitude had been taken by the Christian Churches to the matter of contraception itself.

Are we not taught that our bodies are the temple of the Holy Ghost? If a Christian feels that his or her body is being abused by the un-Christian approach of a supposedly Christian spouse, is it not his duty to 'tell the Church'? Is it not then the Church's duty to seek for a Christian remedy? This might just as well take the form of a rebuke to the partner who insists on a type of sexual practice contrary to the other partner's conscience as it might take the form of exhorting a woman to protect herself against the selfishness and domineering aggressiveness of a too demanding husband.

In the days of the crusades, Christian men considered it their simple duty to don armour and offer their life's blood in the cause of rescuing the holy places from the occupation of the Infidel. Yet what holier place *can* there be than the body of a Christian woman? Where is the modern counterpart of the knight-in-shining-armour who will fight to rescue that holy place from the modern 'Turk' – the Christian husband who is not a Christian?

To the failure of the Christian Churches as a whole to enter realistically and positively into the spiritual problems of the married must be ascribed the massive 'falling away' of the multitude.

For many, the abandonment of religious practice reflects a true loss of faith in a God who has apparently nothing to offer His children but the stones of a lifeless dogma. For many others, this outward abandonment of religious practice is the sign of an inward renewal, a 'going it alone' in the spiritual life, which shows a spirit that augurs well for the future.

How many saints are now hidden from view, awaiting the hour of their manifestation?

To get back, however, to the subject of this chapter, the woman's dilemma in general, it must be borne in mind that *had* women been able to solve on their own this problem of conceptions more numerous than their human strength can bear, solve it say by a simple means of their own devising, then there would never have been this particular birth control controversy. The whole matter would have remained as much a woman's private business as is the management of her own menstrual periods. But, of course, life is not so simple and contraceptives are not, on the whole, found growing upon trees.

Like any other manufactured article, they need to be devised, modified, developed, distributed, and sold. This means financial investment, scientific research, competitive development, advertising, specialist knowledge of all kinds, in fact the whole hoo-ha of modern big business. Big business is public business, and thus do moralists and theologians find themselves involved. From this source must needs come attitudes, doctrines and edicts. Thus do consciences form, develop, become more complex and thus does this modern dilemma arise. Roman Catholic theologians, viewing the whole problem through the rosy spectacles of theory, unappreciative of the physical problems, have now tied themselves to an attitude they might well wish they could abandon if such could be achieved without loss of face.

But here it behoves women to be very watchful indeed. Inescapable biological factors have combined with an innate tendency to arrogance in the male to ensure the complete physical subjection and moral slavery of the female. If now the hour of her delivery strikes, let her ensure that no one steals the victory from her when it is already within her grasp. Women must wake up now and consider where they stand in this matter, for it is certain that efficient methods of birth control will work the biggest revolution in her life since the day of her disgrace in the Garden of Eden. But if she is not very watchful, male arrogance will use this very knowledge to further her moral enslavement.

Let it be established, by all means, that sex is inevitable, that sex within the context of monogamous and indissoluble union is the best, that children must still be born within this union and only in such numbers as are within the capacity of the woman to bear.

But, and this is a big but, who is going to make this assessment of capacity? The clergy? The husband? The family doctor? It can be predicted with certainty that all of these will be coming forward to stake their claim as the final arbiter, and if woman fails to put her foot down now it is certain that her last state will be worse than her first. Are we going to allow the world (still a man's world) to say that physically suited as women may be for bearing children, intellectually and morally she is not of a high enough standard to have a say in the number and occasion of her conceptions?

This type of thing was said about female emancipation, about women entering the professions, about women's rights of property ownership, about women's right to vote. Has any improvement in women's lot come about as the result of what men have magnanimously decided to grant her? Has she not rather had to fight a desperate battle on every issue?

Women are not being fanciful when they demand the right to determine how their bodies are used. It is not for the abolition of sex, let all men note now, that they are fighting, but for their right to use heaven-sent techniques to control the otherwise inevitable consequences of even sex in moderation.

To this end the Family Planning Association have been pointing the way for some time now.

It is interesting to note that the inspiration behind this movement gained its original impetus from the Feministic Movement. It was discovered that in this field the Feministic spirit ran at once into a dilemma that served to modify it. If women are going to have careers *and* the number of children that their maternal nature demands, then they must needs have husbands and homes in which to keep these husbands happy. The male requires to be studied and his needs attended to. His basic need is soon discovered to be, once again, sex. Your liberated feminist with her vote, her education, her legal rights and her dutch cap, is found to take an altogether fresh and original view of male sexuality. All the signs indicate that she finds it quite well to her liking.

CHAPTER VIII

THE CATHOLIC WOMAN'S PROBLEM

So it happens that at this particular point in the history of the human race women's basic position is altered. The influences that have hitherto moulded her psyche no longer have the power of an inescapable reality, for reality itself has undergone a change. There is no longer any need for her to adopt herself to that pitiless law of demand and supply: the male demand for sex that results in a production-belt supply of babies. From this she can be liberated, and for better or worse hers is now the choice, whether or not to adapt herself to the new kind of life that opens out before her. She now suddenly and at last has the opportunity of achieving her true freedom.

Freedom is never easy. It imposes its own discipline. In the days when there was no such thing as a reliable contraceptive, and incidentally in the same era of extraordinarily high mortality rates among mothers and babies, women simply had babies. No one thought any less of them for jeopardising their lives. There was no responsibility attached. It was just the way things were.

Since the advent of reliable birth control methods, there are so many things that a woman has to consider. For instance, is now the right time to start a family? Can the family economy stretch to another child? Does she herself want another baby? What does her husband want and why does he want it? How far ought she allow herself to be guided by his views? How far *can* she allow herself to be guided by them? How much does the community need the services she can render, provided she is not having a baby? How much of her attention are her present children in need of? These are but some of the things a woman must consider as she views her responsibility to her marriage in particular and to society at large.

An honest decision has to be arrived at. Then, if she does decide on a baby, she enters the state of pregnancy with her eyes open. It is a voluntary decision to become a mother. At no moment need the new life within her be resented, rather can it be loved and cherished from the very outset.

To help a woman to arrive at a valid decision, in view of the extremely complex factors involved, common sense and religion alike must needs be at her side.

It is at this juncture that the present dilemma of Catholic women is so painfully spotlighted. For a Roman Catholic woman is obliged not only to face these problems alone, but to face them in the teeth of influences that are doing everything in their power to rob her of what little self confidence she possesses.

Women adhering to other religious denominations, or to secular societies – communists, atheists, humanists – have all been helped gradually to adapt to the new circumstances by the quiet background support of those men in their societies who have come to see how important this issue is. Roman Catholic women receive no help whatsoever from the men of their Church, hindrance perhaps, but help no.

It is largely thanks to the great human interest in and sympathy with the problem shown by so many non-Catholics, both as individuals and through their various organisations, and particularly through the work of the Family Planning Association in this country, that many Catholic women have been able to retain their sanity and sense of proportion. If these non-Roman Catholic organisations displayed any of that holier-than-thou attitude to sexual problems that is the peculiar hall-mark of the orthodox Roman Catholic approach, then indeed this problem would have reached crisis proportions long before now. And the crisis would have taken a far more virulent and disruptive form.

The most refreshing aspect of the non-Roman Catholic approach to these problems, for one experiencing it for the first time, is the capacity of the individuals concerned to effortlessly draw upon a seemingly limitless fund of human compassion. Nor is there, seemingly, any tendency to 'crow' over their capitulated opponents.

In a strictly Roman Catholic atmosphere, the approach, if indeed one can call it that, is entirely negative. A woman living in this atmosphere experiences the sensations of being enmeshed in a trap. She desires to be a responsive and loving wife to her husband, and her religion tells her that she ought, it also tells her that the resulting children are an expression of God's will for her. Society tells her that she can only work this theory within the framework of her own physical and economic resources, and she comes to realise that this is so. If her devotion to her husband results in more pregnancies than she can support, she is condemned by society at large and by her own doctor in particular for acting irresponsibly. If she protects herself by the use of contraceptives, she is condemned by her spiritual advisers for 'gross immorality'. If she seeks a solution by avoiding her husband's embraces, she is accused by him of sexual coldness and by her religious advisers for putting him into the way of temptation to adultery.

So in the eyes of the three men who have such an important part to play in her life, her husband, her confessor, her family doctor, she will find herself condemned by one or the other whatever she does. She is called sexually inadequate, wicked, or insane. If it is not really her nature to be the first, and she finds she cannot afford the luxury of the last, then she must needs opt for the second, and decide to become 'wicked'. 'Wickedness' is a concept of herself that she *can* live with, madness and domestic disharmony she cannot.

But what does this condition of 'moral badness' mean to her in relation to her adaptation to life? A Catholic women who is driven by necessity along the path that leads to contraceptive practice finds herself in a position of spiritual isolation. Neither comfort nor sense nor hope is to be obtained from the exponents of her religion. In the pious literature that she has hitherto comforted herself by reading she will find statements like the following: 'The one who sins by lust . . . by practising contraception in any form . . . puts on the face of Ingratitude. Is it any wonder that God has no place in Heaven for those who use His gifts to insult Him? Can anyone doubt that there has to be a Hell for those who throw God's gifts back into His face by their unrepented mortal sins?' (*The Five Faces of Mortal Sin*, by D. F. Miller C.S.R. 1962.)

In this atmosphere she finds all the moral props upon which she has hitherto supported her personality suddenly withdrawn. She experiences something akin to what the lepers of old must have felt when they first detected signs of the disease on their bodies. In her natural desire to avoid the resulting public disgrace, she may go to almost any lengths to hide the truth of what she is doing, from herself and others. She is obliged by fear to live a lie. Others will try to seek some stability, by believing that their leprosy is real and can be best cured by weekly confession of the fact of their sinfulness in this matter. For indeed, as long as she presents the problem as a disease of her own soul, the Roman Catholic clergy are only too glad to accommodate her, but the absolution they give is conditional upon the promise 'that she will never do it again'. If she receives absolution on these terms, whilst having every intention of doing it again then the absolution is invalid and her subsequent Communions 'blasphemous'. To avoid this pitfall, she must frantically convince herself that her contrition is real, and try to receive Holy Communion before her husband's marital energies overtake her new-found sorrow. Indeed, her position is humiliating and her spiritual degradation complete.

Others, on the other hand, will say to themselves: 'All right, if these men *say* I am a leper, then I might as well become one in earnest. If I am to be hanged for a lamb, then why not for a sheep?' Catholic women are not basically more prone to the temptations of adultery than any other women, but having been stripped of all confidence in their own worth by the solid wall of incomprehension with which their problems are met, they are rendered particularly prone to total moral collapse. This scourge is then visited upon the next generation, for a mother who is herself uncertain of what is right and wrong in the question of sexual behaviour is not in a position to pass on to her daughters principles that carry any real weight. The younger generation sense hypocrisy and evasion in their parents' approach, and are of course led to think either less of their parents as people, or less of that moral code by which their parents profess to live.

Still other Catholic women, of perhaps greater intelligence and moral fibre, simply refuse to bow to this tyrannical yoke, and having once found the burden of their Church's teaching too great to carry, will attempt to free themselves of it by openly turning their back on their Church and setting forth to discover if the world itself does not have something better to offer. The longer and more devoutly they have practised their religion, the more agonising and disruptive does the break become. It leaves them wounded and weakened in their personalities. Reintegration becomes extremely difficult and a great deal of destructive bitterness is liable to remain.

In view of the numerous and formidable dangers that face a Catholic woman at every turn, as she tries to free herself from this trap, so is it to be marvelled at that so many do in fact reach some sort of compromise solution that is compatible with the circumstances of their life. But it is always a solution that in some way or other involves the woman in a compromise with integrity.

CHAPTER IX

THE ROMAN CATHOLIC
PROBLEM GENERALLY

FOR the growing number of Roman Catholics who are beginning to experience the full force of this problem in their own
lives, it is distressing for them to realise that it is the official
line of the Church itself that is all but forcing them to bargain
with their personal integrity. This is indeed a shattering discovery for those who have structured their whole lives on the
validity of their Church's claim. It is a truth that the clergy
themselves can hardly be expected to face when presented in
these stark terms. For when viewed in this light the titles
ascribed to the Roman Catholic Church by the original
Protestant Reformers are seen to be hardly too severe: Anti-
Christ, Great Mother of Harlots, Mystical Babylon, etc. From
the shattering nature of this realisation arises many of the
present most fervent apostasies from the Roman Catholic
Church. From this is derived a great deal of the persuasive
power of the Jehovah's Witnesses, who are here and now on
our doorsteps preaching, with ever increasing success, the
message: 'COME OUT OF HER, MY PEOPLE.'

It is at this point that the hitherto sincere and intellectually
convinced Roman Catholic must needs take a firm grip on
himself. Before allowing himself to be swept away by the
emotional hiatus that accompanies such apocalyptical realisa-
tions, he should, out of fairness to his other self, the self that has
so long and so ardently upheld a contrary thesis, stop and
consider whether the present official 'line' of the Roman
Catholic Church does in fact represent true Catholic doctrine.
It is not without the bounds of possibility that an attitude that
is not in fact true doctrine has become to be represented as
such by the power of the persons who erroneously suppose that
it does.

There are other examples in the Church's history: one of the examples quoted frequently is the doctrine on the intrinsic evil of usury – *in any form* – that was once preached with great fervour and noise by some. Another example, of a more terrible error, was the prominence given at one time to the question of the existence and discovery of witches, to the influence of whom it was at one time theologically fashionable to ascribe every kind of illness and misfortune. The original Dominican witch-hunters had as their authority in their work the Papal Bull of Pope Innocent VIII, which instructed and exhorted them to hunt, throughout Europe and wherever the civil authorities would allow them, those wicked and satanically inspired creatures who, by casting spells and such, were undermining the health and well-being of Christian society. Whether there ever were such people is now a matter of academic interest only, for recent studies of many of these trials have revealed the persons accused of witchcraft to be suffering from nervous maladies that are nowadays recognised and successfully treated. Apart from this aspect of the matter, the whole attitude to evil has undergone such a radical change that even when we do discover in our midst persons who make it their business to conjure up evil spirits we still feel, and are indeed encouraged by our spiritual leaders, that the right attitude for a Christian is merely to steer clear, pray for heavenly protection for ourselves, and enlightenment for the wicked ones. We do not feel obliged to unearth the lair of every mysterious cult, and expose their adherents to ridicule; still less do we feel obliged to convict them, on evidence gained under torture, and then burn them alive in public. But not many years ago a pope thought this was the right thing to do, and most educated Christians agreed with him.

Another and more recent 'error' in official teaching was the Jansenist heresy of the last century, the effects of which are still very apparent and against which many and powerful theological guns have been aimed. This doctrine, which is now officially condemned but in its time was preached with great conviction, teaches that Holy Communion should be very rarely received and then only as a reward for past virtue. The contrary doctrine, which is now official, teaches that Communion is a remedy for sin, was instituted as the food for sinners, and as no

one can ever be worthy of it, all should receive frequently and
without morbid fear. So certain are we now of the correctness
of this teaching that we tend to view with amusement the
spiritual difficulties that the erroneous, yet apparently official,
doctrine caused to its adherents. But for the ordinary faithful,
sitting in their pews on a Sunday morning, listening with
attention to their parish priests telling them that it was spiritually
presumptuous and wrong even to think of approaching the altar
more than once a year, there was nothing amusing about it
at all. This was to them 'good catholic doctrine' which they
must heed under penalty of hell fire. It is probably only thanks
to the absence in those days of dedicated journalists and
television interviewers that no pope was ever trapped into a
public statement upholding the Jansenist viewpoint. If he had
been, and many popes must have been themselves convinced
of the rightness of the Jansenist doctrine, having had it taught
them when they were young, then a first-class row would indeed
have broken out.

The very row which is bursting now upon the Roman
Catholic Church. The basis of the row is not really the validity
of this or that question of moral or religious conduct, but
concerns rather the whole question of authority in the Roman
Catholic Church, and its basis in canon law. This is the fundamental issue of the contemporary religious scene. The issue of
birth control is only relevant in so far as it exposes and high-
lights, in a very dramatic manner, the real flaws in the Roman
Catholic edifice. This public exposure of the flaws in the Roman
Catholic structure attracts the attention of the whole world,
because this particular issue – birth control – is one that everyone is involved in at some point. How the Roman Catholic
Church solves it is going to affect the whole future of the world
and the cause of Christian reunion. Not because without the
permission of the Pope people can't benefit from modern
contraceptive knowledge, for indeed they clearly can and do
and in the teeth of his disapproval. The issue of interest is rather
how the whole hierarchical paraphernalia is going to survive
the massive kick in the teeth it would receive if and when an
official 'about turn' is forced on it.

This then is the problem that torments the mind of your
modern Roman Catholic, who is already convinced of the

necessity for change, and who has overcome the temptation to utter anathemas on this great 'mystical Babylon'.

Those Roman Catholics who do not see the need for change, and who have become firmly convinced of the intrinsic rightness of present official teaching, and who would see change in terms of official apostasy, are also in a position of great internal trial.

The stability of both groups will be greatly helped if they remember that the Roman Catholic Church is very old, and has not survived until the present without having weathered many many crises. That in times past, when scandal and crisis have been the most obvious thing about her life, it was no more comfortable and easy for the people living then than it is now. That the modern crisis appears more critical is partly because of the modern means of communication. In times past, when an eminent Roman Catholic was not sure of himself, he only had to hang on and wait, and events themselves would guide him without any necessity for him to commit himself in public, in advance. Now it is not so easy, for at any moment his telephone can ring, and he finds himself subjected to a barrage of searching questions, on this topic and that. If he should commit himself to as much as a breath of a personal opinion that is not in complete agreement with the orthodox, then he at once becomes a 'personality' and his immediate appearance on television is requested. To back down would suggest lack of sincerity. Nor is this predicament a reflection on the sincerity or good manners of the people who put him into it. Rather is it a true reflection of the extent and fervour of public interest in religious matters generally and particularly where the matter in dispute touches on the question of religious authority.

Most of the people reading our daily newspapers are not churchgoers; nor do they profess to have much interest in theological differences; but let one man or woman challenge the authority of their own religious denomination, and the whole nation becomes breathless, as it were, for news of the outcome. The newspapers, radio and television services knowing, as they do from the letters they receive, of the extent and reality of this interest, oblige the public by following the matter up at once, with every means at their disposal. This means that *any* current intra-denominational dispute takes on a quality of drama for the people engaged in it that was quite unknown to any previous generation. This fact of modern life has to be borne in mind when reviewing the true significance of the present row going on in the Roman Catholic Church on the birth control issue. Theology has not yet learned to adapt itself to the pace of modern living – or rather, shall we say, theologians have not. This is a human and eminently excusable weakness, and does not in itself give valid grounds for a loss of confidence in theology itself.

We have dealt with three aspects of the Roman Catholic dispute over birth control that distinguishes it from any other dispute in the history of the Roman Catholic Church.

1. Reproduction is a basic fact of life itself; there are none who can escape its influence, be they politicians grappling with the problems of a population out-growing its present food supply; or be they social workers harassed by the problems of overcrowding, marital breakdowns and illegitimacy; or simply a man and wife bothered by the realisation that they can scarcely afford the cost of the family that they already have.

2. The fact that the problem it creates for Roman Catholics spotlights the whole question of religious authority, this being a matter of particular interest to the British people with their own unique history of religious controversy.

3. That the whole problem has emerged in its present form very suddenly, and official unpreparedness and embarrassment have been exposed by the intense publicity afforded by modern methods of communication.

Against this background and bearing these factors in mind, it would be good to look now at the origins of the official position, so one may understand better how the present impasse has arisen.

CHAPTER X

ONAN'S SIN

IT is frequently stated by Roman Catholic apologists that the Church has *always* opposed artificial methods of birth control, and that which has been successfully and consistently opposed by philosophers and theologians for the best part of two thousand years cannot suddenly become right. At first sight this argument would appear very powerful, until one comes to look at it a little closer.

What is it *precisely* that has always been condemned? 'Artificial methods of birth control.' But what artificial methods have been known (in the sense of being widely known) before the last 50 years or so? Prior to the turn of this century, a few perhaps used primitive methods of various types, but they were not widely advocated, and are of no significance in this controversy. What in fact the Church has condemned through the ages is birth prevention by means of abnormal sexuality.

Prior to the introduction of the condom and the dutch cap, there was only one way to ensure that conception did not occur, and that was to pervert, in some way, the very nature of the sexual act. The aim of the particular perversion must needs be to prevent the semen entering the vagina, and this could only be achieved by either the penis never entering the vagina, or else being withdrawn prior to seminal emission.

Such acts are justly considered perversions, when one stops to consider the nature of the sexual drive itself, as experienced by the two participants. The personal aim of the act is orgasm, either in oneself or in one's partner, according to the maturity of the relationship. Married people soon realise that solitary orgasm has very little meaning, and the aim of both is ideally that of orgasm in the other. The act as it appears to be designed by nature would seem to give the greatest likelihood of that result being achieved, i.e. by the insertion of the penis in the vagina and its maintenance in that position until emission occurs. Withdrawal before emission must necessarily deprive the female of much chance of achieving vaginal orgasm. Though clitoral orgasm may be still achieved, it is of such a vastly inferior nature that its substitution in one who has experienced the former is not going to be readily accepted. Indeed, why should it? The ability to achieve a vaginal orgasm is a sign of sexual maturity in the female, and it is an ability that men themselves value highly. The habit of interrupted coitus, or withdrawal before emission, is one that militates against sexual stability and happiness, and would seem to be basically unnatural.

N.B. The argument against interrupted coitus, advanced here, is by no means all that can be said against it, the matter will be taken up again later when comparing this method of birth control with other methods. What is written here concerns the objections to the method even when it is the only method available, as it has in fact been through the ages – the one method available to all, understandable by all and THE method that has in fact incurred the displeasure of the theologians.

If the argument of the theologians against *coitus interruptus* is based simply on the assertion that such an act frustrates nature, then no one can argue with them. If one enquires further and asks 'whose nature?' they are rather liable to become a little vague, to start spelling nature with a capital 'N', and talk about the purpose of the act being primarily reproductive.

The simple truth of the matter is that when two persons engage upon an act of sexual intercourse their primary aim is not children but orgasm. If they conduct the act in such a way as to render orgasm virtually impossible for one partner then they are acting so as to frustrate nature – the woman's nature, whose natural desire it is to experience vaginal orgasm with the penis *in situ* until it can remain so no longer.

There is no doubt that the story about Onan in Genesis chapter 38 has had a profound influence on thought on questions of sexual behaviour. It is described there how Onan, in order to avoid conception, spilled his seed upon the ground during intercourse, and was slain by the Lord for the 'detestable thing' that he did. These words are very commonly used to prove that birth control is a detestable thing.

The author leaving Westminster Cathedral on May 31st, 1964. With her is Dr. Iris Tempowsky, Founder of the Independent Catholic Women's Group.

The author speaking to the press and television outside Westminster Cathedral. Some

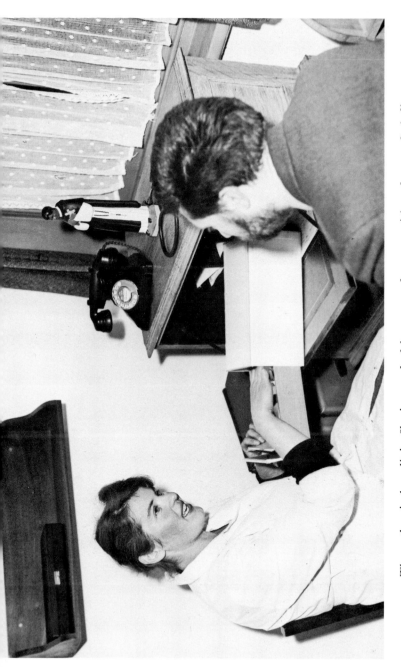

The author in her clinic. She is consulted by men and women, rich and poor, Catholic and non-Catholic. She hopes that the clinic she has opened in her home will be the first of many.

The author with her seven children, near their home in Wallasey

London Daily Herald

n the left: Alexandra (5), Dominic (8), Lucy (3), Victoria (10),
Stephen (7), Nicholas (12), Benedict (13).

A happy family scene. The author with four of her children.

The author off on her rounds.

The author praying in Westminster Cathedral on May 31, 1964, where she received Holy
Communion ... free being deprived of it by her own Bishop and parish priest. Her father ...

Just as easily could the story be used to prove that it is interrupted coitus that is detestable.

The story has certainly been interpreted and reinterpreted by many. The present version is simply given as the way the author sees it:

Onan's brother Er came to a premature death leaving Tamar, his widow, childless. Family pressure was put upon Onan to marry his brother's widow, which was the custom at the time. Children born would then be still considered Er's children, as far as inheritance went. This was not to Onan's liking, and he dealt with the situation as already described.

But what of his wife, Tamar? Tamar then and there required children. She was also, by Onan's advances, led to desire vaginal orgasm. In his intention of depriving her of the former, he was at the same time depriving her of the latter. Probably it was she who killed him. His approach was utterly selfish. If he really had a good reason not to raise up seed to his brother's wife, he could have taken himself elsewhere, but that would have meant he would have lost his bit of fun. So without any consideration for the feelings of the woman whom he was so powerfully arousing with hopes of the children she had not yet had, he went into her, made love to her, aroused her sexual desires, got her to the pitch of great expectation and hope, and then simply spilled his seed upon the ground, and left her alone, thoroughly frustrated and upset, and to face future humiliation by the public reproach of 'barrenness'.

Taken in its most fundamental terms therefore, the Church's condemnation of birth control has meant the *protection* of the sexual integrity of women. For indeed, if there is no other method of birth prevention, it is better to have normal intercourse and many children than to risk the physiological and psychological dangers of marital onanism.

Thus it can be maintained that the Church's position HAS always been right. The only snag is that the men who were responsible for upholding this argument did not, in fact, fully understand it. Not understanding women themselves, they allowed their attention to wander from the needs of women and the nature of women, and found it easier instead to consider nature itself. Some impersonal natural force 'out there', to which all must needs bow down and do homage. They have made of this nature their god and have made it in their own image and likeness. A god who does not love women. They failed to see that in the ban on sexual practice of a kind that deprives a woman of the physical, and hence emotional, completion (the completion that makes intercourse mean something) God has in fact been protecting woman's integrity. Man was made by God in His own image and likeness, woman was made to be man's helpmate. By the centuries-long ban by the Christian Churches on all forms of sex between man and woman that were not both vaginal and complete, human beings have been protected from a perversion of their sexual appetites.

It does so happen that the Roman Catholic Church has been the most vigorous of all in making this point. It also happens that the Roman Catholic Church teaches a unique doctrine about a mystical woman. It seems to the author that there is a close connection between the development of this mystical content and the mental and spiritual opposition put up to the idea of a perverted sexuality in marriage. The astonishing thing at present is the apparent total failure to relate the doctrine of 'the second Eve' to flesh and blood Christian women. It is for the relating of mystical thought to the realities of personal sexual experience that the Roman Catholic Church, and all the theologians in her, must now go into labour.

The theologians have been preaching a doctrine that they have not fully understood and now it is as though Judgement Day itself has come upon them. They are required to stand up in public and reveal their innermost thoughts. They must now bring forth the truth about the sexual implications of their own personal mysticism.

One can see running concurrently through the history of Catholic thought two themes diametrically opposed, yet deriving from the same doctrinal thought. The doctrine in question is the fact of Onan's sin. The deriving themes are:

1. He sinned because he DISOBEYED his father, and REFUSED to lodge his seed in its proper extra-Onan habitat.

2. He sinned because he denied his partner her proper and lawful desire to receive his seed.

The first concept lays stress on OBEDIENCE and NATURAL law.

The second stresses the right of woman to have a say. These
two themes can be traced right through the history of the
Catholic Church. The first is strictly conservative, authoritarian,
official and very well entrenched; it is called by its enemies
'Pharisaical'. The second is liberal, revolutionary even, has
always had a very hard time to get its voice as much as heard
and is called by its enemies 'anarchistical'.

But both themes belong to the Roman Catholic Church,
and both reflect truths about her. The adherents of one viewpoint cannot afford to dismiss the others as 'not truly Roman
Catholic', any more than the participants on either side in a
civil war can afford to dismiss the other side as 'not really our
countrymen'. For they clearly are of the same country, they are
truly present, and victory for neither side is possible until the
other be overcome. So it is in the Roman Catholic Church now,
nothing less than civil war. War that must be fought to the
finish with only death or victory at the end. There is no compromise possible.

The official and entrenched position, viewing the sexual
scene through its own peculiar brand of coloured spectacles,
was quite unprepared to take an objective view of the first
contraceptive devices as they made their appearance at the
beginning of this century. They were seen at once as barricades
set up by rebellious human nature for the purpose of perverting
the law of God, and thus have they been represented ever since,
and with ever-increasing difficulty and embarrassment as the
contraceptives themselves suddenly become less material, less
obstacle like, more physiological. The mental gymnastics
required to defend this position is becoming increasingly
obvious to all, so more and more one sees the defenders bringing
out and relying upon their one heavy gun: 'Birth prevention
by direct interference with the course of nature IS THE SIN OF
ONAN, and the Lord slew Onan for doing A DETESTABLE THING.'

The tendency of the opposing line of thought has been from
the beginning to view the entire problem from the viewpoint
of woman, her nature and her needs. This line of thought has
been all but strangled at birth. Adherents have been persecuted,
silenced and scattered. But they live on. By no means officially
in the Church, for they have discovered that within it they
cannot survive. But yet they know themselves to be still part

of it. They know they are as genuinely Roman Catholic as the people who have cast them out without a trial.

[Should anyone doubt the utterly totalitarian methods employed by the Roman Catholic clergy against the Roman Catholic clergy, then let them consider the following facts: In sex matters every priest in the confessional is faced with certain dreaded canonical penalties. If in confession a priest gives advice or judgement that is not .in keeping with the 'official' tenets in the matter of sex, by canon law the penitent is bound to 'denounce' the said confessor to the Bishop or the Holy Office. If the penitent fails to do this, he (or more probably she) automatically falls into 'excommunication'. A priest who decides in a particular case to take his courage in both hands and decide against an 'Instruction' of the Holy See thereafter must live under a shadow of fear. For should the penitent have future scruples, and ask another confessor for advice on the same issue, mentioning the advice formerly received, this second confessor might feel bound to bind her (under pain of excommunication) to denounce the first priest to his Bishop. This priest might then never be allowed to hear confessions again.]

So it is scarcely to be wondered at that there is such uniformity and solidarity in the ranks of the Roman Catholic clergy. A priest who values his own conscience more than official instructions cannot live in the Roman Catholic Church, he must get out or perish. But though he is 'outside' he is still a priest, and many are there who are even now quietly biding their time, as did David during King Saul's lifetime, awaiting the moment when the Lord will once again restore His inheritance to Israel.

The hour they await is the hour of the battle for the vindication of 'the woman' whose needs they understand and whose rights they so passionately defend.

CHAPTER XI

THE ROMAN CATHOLIC SIN

REMEMBER the verse of G. K. Chesterton: 'For we are the people of England, and we haven't spoken yet'? That line contains both a warning and a prophecy. Let us now look further into this matter, for it is a great matter and one worthy of being looked into.

This is not a battle of kings and princes, this is the battle of the common folk and the little people. It is THEIR battle; the issue is their right to be themselves; the sources of the conflict are their own secret nightmares; the outcome is to be one that expresses the might of the living God within them.

Let us pause for a moment and consider once again just what is entailed when a woman enters the state of matrimony (by which I mean Christian marriage as we have been brought to understand). Volumes without number have been written on this subject, in terms ranging from the highest romantic idealism to the hardest facts about legal rights. From one extreme to the other, some contribution could be made here, but rather does it seem necessary to confine the matter to the boundaries relevant to Roman Catholics and birth control.

So in this chapter I have in mind the present-day Roman Catholic wife, who has to contend with all the troubles that all married women faced in a bygone age, but troubles now, for her, magnified a hundredfold.

In this age there are legalities that safeguard a woman's property when she marries, no longer does all her property and rights over such automatically pass to her husband. There are also some civil regulations that safeguard her person. But despite these she still (by the definition of Christian marriage) has to concede the right of access to her body to her husband. Once conceded, at the wedding ceremony, the power of the Church enforces her everlasting acquiescence to his sexual appetite. This means sexual intercourse whenever he wants it.*

Not only are there social pressures towards fewer and 'better' children, but also modern medicine is saving the lives of many babies that would, at one time, have been born dead, or died soon after birth. This means that earlier and earlier in marriage a woman is under pressure from society at large, and from the needs of the family she already has, to limit her conceptions.

There is no natural and automatic resulting limitation upon her husband's sexual drive. With this she is now well and truly walled up. There is no corresponding social pressure put upon her husband to bring this drive under control. Society at large (non-Catholic society) has found its own solutions, and nowhere any way along the line has any serious consideration been given to the question of developing a pill for men which would have the effect of modifying a normal man's sexual desire. Nor has the Church come to the wife's assistance by preaching a fervent crusade for male sexual restraint in marriage. The Catholic woman finds herself quite on her own.

The obvious male solution is abnormal sexuality.

Here let it be noted that *coitus interruptus* is but the most innocent of the possible perversions. There is no intention of listing the number and nature of the alternatives here. Suffice it to say that this can be read to include every kind of unnatural and degrading sexual practice that men can devise to inflict upon women. It is not necessarily implied that such lengths are always gone to, but the possibility is there, the door has been opened. Habit in sexual practice is one that rapidly develops, and affects the entire orientation of the personality, and is indeed just as grave a matter as moralists have always maintained. Within the framework of modern Roman Catholic marriage, there is a great temptation for some men to try to seek their solutions along the lines of such perversions of normal appetite. By confining their activities to their wife, they can convince themselves that this still has something to do with 'holy matrimony'.

There is of course another type of man, probably far

* Catholics sometimes say: 'But the Church allows separation.' This answer simply begs the question, and indeed is a kind of mockery. So often, when the need for separation is most strongly felt, the woman is at her most physically, emotionally and financially dependent, that is, directly after child-birth.

commoner, who would not care to force such perversions on his wife, and would prefer to find his own relief in solitary sexuality. The greater the difficulty he experiences in approaching his wife, the greater will be the tendency to seek this solution. It is a solution that causes men a great deal of unhappiness, they feel their hearts all but shrivelling up, under its prolonged influence, but they do not know what to do. None of the advice given to the unmarried who are faced with this problem is applicable here. Who IS in the position to counsel a married man as to the right thing to do with his sexual drive, when suddenly, within marriage and after a habit of frequent and normal intercourse has developed, he suddenly finds himself morally obliged to no longer touch the woman at his side? If some women have had inflicted on them all the plagues of hell, walled up alive as they are with their husband's sexuality, so have many men, without a doubt, experienced a torture of another kind, and borne it in patience without inflicting their essential incontinence upon their wives.

A wife may be insensitive to the need of a husband, when hidden in this manner. She can scarcely remain indifferent in the former case, when she herself is in danger of becoming the object of the perversion.

To protect herself from this kind of perversion, the 'good wife' has only one weapon, and that is the ready offering of vaginal coitus, and an insistence that nothing less will be tolerated.

In this act she also needs to participate fully, in order to transform the act from a manifestation of male lust into an act of mutual love. For though the motive of this act is derived from a body other than her own, hers alone is the power to sanctify it. And hers the guilt if she fails. For if she fails to make this offering of herself and attempts to withhold lawful access to her body from its rightful owner (by lawful is meant vaginal), then she is laying the door wide open to the introduction into the marriage of every kind of intra and extra marital perversion. This has always been well understood by Catholic moralists. What is not (apparently) understood is that there is no power on this earth that can protect a woman from her husband's sexual advances and no power that can ensure that these advances will in fact be vaginal in intention.

Right, let a woman understand at the outset that sexual stimulation will be her lot in marriage, and let her insist from the outset that all contact MUST be (primarily) vaginal, there is still nothing that can prevent withdrawal from taking place, before the act is completed. The combination of the fear of pregnancy and the habit of vaginal coitus (in the absence of an efficient contraceptive technique) would seem to point to one inevitable outcome, that of interrupted coitus.

Celibate theologians seem to be of the opinion that all that is required is knowledge of Catholic teaching plus a determination to work it and, hey presto, the problem is solved. Why do priests suppose that total sexual abstinence is possible for a man? Sometimes they quote their own celibacy as proof of its possibility. They are then liable to be asked how many times they have themselves shared a bed with a member of the opposite sex and at the same time abstained from sexual intercourse? The question is, of course, as absurd as the argument that provoked it. A married man is a man who has a wife. This wife represents the totality of his physical, emotional and financial investment. She also happens to be at his side at the moment in question. According to the measure of his past faithfulness to this wife of his, so is his house filled with her children, and there is no other bed to which he might betake himself. His conscious waking mind might tell him that tonight, anyway, there should be no sex. But in the early hours of the morning the effects of sleep and feminine proximity are felt. Erection is what begins to happen. Intercourse with withdrawal at the moment of emission seems to be the obvious solution, and like as not, is what in fact occurs.

The mental processes that accompany this event take the following lines: 'I know the Church condemns this, but God knows, I can't help it. At least I've done my best to see that my wife will not conceive, any guilt is mine. I'll mention it next time in confession. Anyway, I feel better now.' And with that he goes off to sleep.

The present fuss in the Roman Catholic Church about the unlawfulness of contraceptive devices, combined as it is with the social fuss about Catholic women needing to have fewer children, tend to simply precipitate a greater number of unsatisfactory, and strictly unnatural sexual acts. Vague guilt may be felt, but very few are the men who seem to be unduly troubled by this deception. From their point of view indeed the method can become increasingly attractive. There is some sadistic pleasure to be gained from the tension and anxiety the practice arouses in the woman; on the whole it seems to work – the wife doesn't in fact conceive so often; there is no incriminating paraphernalia; his own sexual tension is released; it is definitely more fun than masturbation; the feelings of guilt that do result are not so heavy that they cannot be borne from one occasional confession to another. So there is no break with his Church and all seems well.

Some wives indeed have become so conditioned by this treatment that they seem to expect nothing better. Sexual satisfaction is something they come to forget the meaning of. Their resulting lack of interest in sex is seriously equated with 'purity' and the man's efficiency at working the method is equally seriously equated with 'self-control'. Such a couple can really convince themselves that they are living a good clean Catholic life. No undue emphasis on sex in their house! No nasty wicked 'special precautions'! and is not the priest always at hand to wash away any misgivings? That is of course provided the facts are presented with a suitable display of 'contrition'. Such contrition is not difficult to produce, for indeed sex to such people has become such a bore, that they really and truly wish they could have nothing more to do with it. But, of course, physiology overtakes them, and on and on they muddle. Such an approach *might* carry a couple through to a decent Catholic burial ground, or it *might* end in disaster of another nature. Just say one or other of the partners in this parody of marriage suddenly and surprisingly meets with a second romantic encounter? Such things *have* been known to happen. . . .

This is the nightmare behind the façade of solid marital comfort. This ogre has always been there, ready to swallow the spiritually casual, but in times past it did not arise so often because the fear of pregnancy was not so widespread. Most women had big families, it was accepted as natural; everyone helped everyone else, and the temptation to practise interrupted coitus was not on the whole so strong.

Now, as has already been explained, the temptation for Catholics has never been stronger, and could not be stronger. The more intelligent know quite well that in the Church's eyes the practice is condemned on the same basis as any of the more sane and efficient methods, so on the principle that they might as well be hanged for a sheep as a lamb they proceed to fit themselves up accordingly. And being more intelligent, they soon realise that the weekly game of contrition and absolution is for them nothing less than hypocrisy, and gradually and in ever increasing numbers they are refusing to play it. But they know it is not their Catholic faith they are turning their back upon. It is spiritual totalitarianism that they are refusing to bow and scrape and fawn to. This is the origin of the present revolt.

But finally, what of the less intelligent, the less well informed, the impoverished masses of poor Catholic countries? In such countries there are no devices to be obtained. The power of the Church sees to that. For such people interrupted coitus remains the ONLY solution. Thus the Roman Catholic Church, by her failure to understand the real nature of Onan's sin, has forced her own children to embrace it. The result is that total spiritual corruption that is the norm within the Roman Catholic Church today.

Nothing is now what it seems. The 'pure' are the hypocrites. The honest and forthright are the 'scandalous apostates'. How long can this last?

So far this chapter has confined itself to the social and moral evils resulting from the practice of interrupted coitus. But what are its effects on the female psyche? It may be a practice that is imposed on her, against her will, in a deliberate attempt to deprive her of the children she truly desires. Or it may be a practice that she insists her husband uses in order to protect herself from the effects of a sexual contact that she doesn't want. Whatever reasons lie behind its adoption, it is a practice that she experiences as a belittling of her own femininity. 'He uses me as he would a lavatory' is her own secret comment. She knows that in agreeing to such a practice she is agreeing to something that makes her less of a person, not more. She wonders what the meaning of 'sacrament' can possibly be in such a marital context It becomes obvious to her that she has missed her vocation as a virgin. Virgins do not have anything like this to contend with night in and night out: sexual stimulation followed by total frustration at the moment of climax. If she, the wife, consents, for the sake of peace, she is consenting to her own future neurosis. If she does not consent, she is either driving her man to seek his relief elsewhere, or else she is obliging him to complete the act, and by the doing of this bringing down many curses upon her own head. The curse of unwanted pregnancy; the illnesses and weaknesses of pregnancy; the particular horror of pregnancy with a man of whom she is perhaps no longer sure; and, most bitter pill of all, the reproach: 'It's all your fault, you should have let me do it MY way.'

It is probably better for a woman to consent to the logical conclusion of the act of love, accepting the associated risks, than to be a party to its unnatural thwarting. *Coitus interruptus*, when the result of ignorance and spiritual terror, is an abortion of sex, and manages to be the negation of love, life, marriage, religion – all rolled into one.

For if the woman agrees to it for the sake of avoiding pregnancy, she has no assurance that it has been successful. The duration of the sex act, that is no more than a parody of the sex act, is spent in anxious speculation as to whether he will withdraw in time. And time thereafter, until her next period, must be spent in waiting to discover whether her fears were justified.

This particular question, for a woman approaching the menopause, takes on a particularly agonising aspect. For not only is pregnancy so late on particularly dreaded, but her periods are anyway particularly irregular. Sex itself comes to be experienced as a refined kind of physical torture, the rest of her waking hours is a prolonged form of mental torture. Any Catholic priest will tell her that it is still better for her to put up with these things (if her marital situation is such that she cannot prevent her husband having intercourse with withdrawal), than for her to insert a remedy purchased at the chemist, which would at least serve to lessen her anxiety. We are taught that God is just. I wonder what penalty He has in store for those men who have sat by, and watched without apparently any misgivings as to their own rectitude, this prolonged and senseless torturing of middle-aged women?

But for the younger, more robust wife and one who has perhaps a measure of influence with her husband, it is better for her to agree to any number of pregnancies with ALL their accompanying sorrow than to agree to this practice.

We are supposing now, of course, that there is no other remedy available. So she resists this practice and brings many sorrows on her own head, and on no account should she look anywhere for consolation, for there is none to be had. The priest will tend to assume that she is doing no more than her simple duty, and should that duty appear too onerous, he is capable of remarking, with some display of irritation, that the remedy is in her own keeping, and that she should learn 'self-control'. What does he mean by this? It is quite obvious that he does not know what he means. If he means that she should learn to encourage her husband to practise withdrawal, why doesn't he say so? Because he cannot say so, because he knows that such a practice is not only contrary to common sense and common physiology, but is also contrary to what the Church has faithfully taught through the ages, which is that *coitus interruptus* is wrong. Another answer that the pious (and usually unmarried) will produce is 'the example of the Virgin Mary'. As she remained always a virgin (according to Catholic doctrine) she obviously had the key to a happy married life. According to this line of thought, all a married woman need do, who is bothered by sexual problems, is to invoke her aid. 'She was pure and had no problems, you have problems, therefore you are NOT pure,' so runs the argument. This line of thought, very common in the Catholic Church, is frankly stating that the measure of a person's sexual problems is a measure of their impurity. Can one wonder at the number of wives, who on hearing this, take one gulp, and opt henceforth for the company of the pure? Sex and all the problems of personality associated with its right development and use are simply buried alive into the depths of the psyche, and a heavy door is slammed on them. 'Keeping the faith' comes to mean nothing more than keeping this door firmly closed. Sex becomes then merely something not very nice, that married women have done to them in the dark.

This is the ultimate position of fetid horror that the priests have brought their people to. But we have already seen that the priests are themselves by no means free agents. It is the authoritarianism and totalitarianism of the Roman canon law that has worked this outrage on reason, truth and religion alike.

Once again must we stop and thank our 'separated brethren' for their kindliness towards us, and for simply being there. If it were not for them we would all be a good deal crazier than we are.

But, at the same time, let us remember that the Roman Catholic Church is God's Church, or so we have always believed. Why should we cease to believe because we discover that the minds of the Church's leaders have been clouded with darkness? This darkness must be for a reason. It could be that we have to experience this darkness from without, so that we shall be obliged to look for the light that comes from within. It could be that we need to experience this rule of satanic darkness, so that we will recognise with greater surety the kingdom of God, when it appears in our midst. Those who say that Roman Catholics who do not accept the Church's ruling on birth control should leave the Church (and there are many more non-Catholics who say this than Catholics) do not appear to know much about God's dealings with His people.

When the Lord wished to afflict Israel, what did He do? Time and again His visiting scourge took the form of a bad ruler. Was he not angry with Israel for wanting a king at all? Did He not send them Saul, whom He then afflicted with madness, and who in turn afflicted his people? And for the course of the appointed time during which the affliction was to last, was He not anointing David to be His people's King?

Have we not good reason to suppose that God is angry with the people of the Roman Catholic Church (His people, as it happens) for all their sins of past complacency? Who has a religion like unto our religion? has been our boastful query for many a long day. If we had spent as long on our knees trying to understand the truths of our own religion, studying Christ's approach to people and trying to imitate it at no matter what cost to ourselves, would we then have found it necessary to gawk after authority and plead for guidance from Rome? Would not Rome itself have reformed itself long ago, if Roman Catholics had been the kind of people it was worth bothering to reform anything for? These are the questions we would do well to ask ourselves, before murmuring against God for having afflicted us with such spiritual darkness. The Roman Catholic Church has been for us as the sun itself, the source of all light, the source of all warmth and hope. If the sun has now gone into total eclipse, and we find ourselves shivering in the dark and cold, does that make our past knowledge of the sun's glory delusional? Does it not rather make us realise with gratitude how great is the gift of the sun's light and how wondrous it will seem when it shines once more? It appears to Roman Catholics indeed that God has forsaken His people. He has sent us leaders that lead us nowhere but into further darkness. But is there not a David awaiting his hour?

While we wait and endure our humiliations, we can at least be spending our time in reflections upon matters that touch on personal integrity and truth, and learning what we can from those dogmas of our faith that are peculiarly our own, about which the non-Catholic world knows nothing.

CHAPTER XII

A TWENTIETH-CENTURY SOLUTION

IT has been shown that the basis of marital peace is the self-sacrificing devotion of the wife to the cause of sexual harmony. This work is woman's true work in this world. Her task in times past when society needed her babies was onerous and often heart-breaking, and left her no time or opportunity to develop her talents for anything else, but for all that the demands on her were straightforward.

With the advent of the industrial revolution the need for women in industry, the shortage of living space, etc., her task became more difficult, as her duties became more numerous. The shadow of 'family limitation' by the only means known (interrupted coitus) fell across her path. With the advent of education for women, vast new fields opened up before her. The more adventurous founded the 'Family Planning Move-ment' with contraceptives newly discovered, solving the basic sexual problem. Society came to expect more and more of women. If they were to marry at all, they found more and more their choice lying between a total sacrifice of their new-found position in society, or the establishment of a small planned family and the continuance of their careers. In educated non-Catholic circles, this became more and more the pattern of advance, with their example showing the way to others. The approach of the Roman Catholic Church to this question has been throughout quite negative, and Roman Catholic women have been caught in the cross streams of social changes and negative spiritual counsel. In this atmosphere, and without any support from the men of their religion, they have had to fight a desperate battle for survival. Any success they have achieved has been won at the expense of their religious integrity. If this lost ground is to be made up, then it is the men of the Roman Catholic Church who require to move now and move fast towards a recognition of the basic rights of women. Their right to their sexual integrity in marriage, and their spiritual right to responsible motherhood, which recognises that the number and occasion of her conceptions is a matter that remains the prime responsibility for every woman to discover for herself.

It has been shown that the opposition to these advances put up by the Roman Catholic Church is based upon a false assessment of the value of sex itself, combined with a failure to understand the meaning of the female contribution. It has been shown how the negative state of mind, induced by this opposition, has spread like a dark cloud over the entire Roman Catholic horizon, and how it has come to pass that now all the signs point to the imminence of a great spiritual conflict, a battle concerning the fundamental dignity of woman and her position in the newly structured Catholic Church that will emerge from the ashes of the old. This conflict is to be one that will dispel this gloom for good and re-establish certainty and hope once more in the new kind of world that opens up before all mankind.

What is going to be the particular characteristic of this New World? It will be a society that recognises sex as good in itself and that without reference to reproduction. It will be revealed that with sex viewed aright marriage will become right, and will create for itself the right atmosphere for the bringing forth of children. Children who will be first wanted and then conceived. Not conceived first and then perhaps wanted, which is the mode of the coming into the world of nearly every one of us. The new style must needs bring forth a new kind of child. For, 'Behold,' saith the Lord, 'I make all things new'.

But let it not be forgotten that this idyllic state of affairs, the state in which every child born is a wanted child, can only come about when all have refashioned their attitudes to sex, and when all understand clearly their duties to each other, within the social framework. Thus the work of re-education remains formidable. There is nothing to stop the Roman Catholic clergy themselves undertaking this work. Are they not indeed ideally suited? With their disciplined lives, their freedom from personal marital obligations, their total dedication to the ideal of building God's kingdom on earth? But before they can begin to undertake this work they must first emerge from the cloud under which they are now hidden. They must be re-educated themselves, throw off the old attitudes along with the old shackles that bound them, and re-emerge as a new kind of Christian man. A man who carries Christ with him and moves as freely as the Son of God Himself about this world, which is destined to become the dwelling place of God. For is it not written: 'Here is God's tabernacle pitched among men; he will dwell among them and they will be his own people and He will be among them, their own God.'

Whether the Catholic clergy are capable of rising to these heights remains to be seen, but anyway the challenge is there for them to make of what they will. That they will indeed fulfil their destiny in this way would seem, to the author of this book, to be written upon their foreheads.

However, for their contribution we must needs wait. In the meantime the rest of us must forge ahead with the work that is at hand waiting to be done. One of the basic ingredients of knowledge in the new society, is going to be, of necessity, and by definition, an absolutely reliable contraceptive technique.

So the time has come now in this work to review the methods at present available.

METHODS

In the first place it would be good to summarise what the basic necessary qualities are, in the opinion of the author, for a contraceptive method to possess in order to qualify as a good method.

1. There must be no interference with the individual act, in such a manner as to render it more difficult for either partner to achieve orgasm.

2. The method must be one of sufficiently proved reliability, to abolish anxiety, as far as is possible. The purpose of the individual sexual act is the maximum sexual satisfaction of the partners. Their mutual confidence in the method must be such that their attention should not be distracted by it.

3. As the MOST interested partner (in the question of reliability) is the woman, the ideal method is one that she has herself, within her own keeping, as it were.

4. The method should be as free as possible from any harmful side effects.

Bearing these factors in mind, we will now review the present available methods.

Coitus Interruptus

1. In the course of this method, the act itself is seriously interfered with. By its use it is difficult, if not impossible, for the woman to achieve an orgasm at all. The quality of the male orgasm is reduced by the concentration required to ensure that withdrawal occurs before emission.

2. The method has no proved reliability at all. Any possibility of success depends entirely on the degree of concentration given to the method itself, at the time of its application. Interrupted coitus is not coitus. The most 'successful' act of its kind cannot be more than a coitus that has been successfully interrupted.

3. The woman has no control over this method at all. If it fails, it is the woman who bears the effects of the failure, and it is certain that her full wrath must be visited upon her husband. A more than usually unhappy atmosphere in which to embark upon yet another unwanted pregnancy.

4. This method is notorious for the number and gravity of its harmful side effects, ranging from neuroses of all kinds to marital disharmony of the worst kind.

Against these considerations, and in all fairness, it must be now stated that there are some couples who have practised this method for years with complete success and with no resulting marital disharmony whatsoever. Such people are usually found to be exceptional with a very deep fund of love and respect for each other. So it must be admitted that it is possible to work this method without loss or danger to the quality of the marriage, but such cases are rare. In most marriages deep respect and affection of the order required to make a success of this method of birth control are simply not present at the outset, when a reliable method might be the thing the marriage needs most. Thus it is not a method that can be recommended to any seeking advice. That older people might come to see in it an answer to their particular problems is a different matter altogether. To such people, who are BOTH happy in what they do, no one else can possibly have any criticism.

The Safe Period

This method is also known as 'the Rhythm method', or 'Periodic Abstinence'. The method is based on the theory that ovulation in the female occurs only once a month, at a certain predictable time in the monthly cycle. Male sperm are able to live in the female genital tract for a number of days, so intercourse must be avoided for that number of days *before* ovulation is expected to take place. The egg itself is viable for a number of days after discharge from the ovary, and therefore intercourse must be avoided for that number of days *after* ovulation is supposed to have occurred. These days, taken all together, constitute 'the fertile period'. The remaining time, i.e. approx. 1 week before menstruation, the duration of menstruation itself, and anything from 1 to 5 days after its completion, constitute 'the infertile period', or 'safe period'. 'Safe' in this context means safe for sexual intercourse without conception.

Before this method can be worked, it is necessary for the woman to be in possession of knowledge relating to the state of her fertility at any particular time. This knowledge can only be gained, for any particular cycle, from a study of past cycles. The event of ovulation itself is found to be commonly associated with a rise in basal body temperature. By taking her temperature on waking each morning for a period of several months, and by charting the results, a study of these charts will tell the woman when to anticipate ovulation in the current cycle. Another method of calculation does not rely upon temperature charts, but on a record of a large number of cycle lengths, from which can be calculated the mean ovulatory time, with a plus and minus each side, to account for the known variations.

Some women menstruate with almost clockwork regularity, and are never in any doubt as to where they are in their cycle. Others are normally very irregular, so much so that calculation becomes extremely difficult and not a little hazardous. Some women ovulate with almost clockwork regularity and know, from various observable signs – other than the rise in morning temperature – exactly when they are doing so. But even so, for any particular cycle, the calculation of how many days abstinence is necessary *before* ovulation must of necessity be based on the assumption that ovulation this month will indeed take place at the anticipated time.

Whatever the method of approach, several months of total sexual abstinence are required in order to collect the information from which a reliable prediction can be made.

Many women who would like to use this method are prevented by their inability to win this period of reprieve for themselves, and have indeed conceived before they have been able to collect sufficient data. The 'safe period' technique depends upon the menstrual flow as its guide line. When the flow disappears, as can happen during or after severe illness, for variable periods of time after child-birth, or simply for no apparent reason whatsoever, then the method becomes unworkable, and total abstinence must replace periodic.

Another disadvantage is that nervous shock, emotional upset or even an attack of influenza, not to mention sexual excitation, can all serve to precipitate ovulation. A number of 'safe-period' failures can be ascribed to this cause.

Very little is in fact known regarding the factors that control ovulation, even less is known about the exact duration of viability of different types of spermatozoa in different feminine environments. A great deal more remains to be discovered before the method can be relied upon to any great extent.

For all this, however, the fact remains that many couples do succeed in working this method with great efficiency and have developed great confidence in it. In the cases where a cycle can be established and confidence in the method has not been undermined by past failure, then the method looked at purely as a contraceptive measure at the time of its application is a good one.

Examination under the previous four headings reveals the following:

1. There is no interference with the orgasmal potentiality of the individual act.

2. Calculations having already been made, sexual activity is instigated in an atmosphere of confidence and no distraction is created by the method itself in the course of the act. (That is, provided the woman does not believe that sexual excitation can precipitate ovulation.)

3. The very fact that the method is being used shows that the woman already has control of the situation, both as regards knowledge of her own physiological state and the ability to see that her husband recognises these states, and is willing to abstain accordingly.

4. The question of resulting harm is a more subtle one alto-

gether. Not only does the method itself imply sexual abstinence, in most cases for as much as half of the monthly cycle, but it also requires total abstinence for the number of months required to gather together sufficient knowledge of the ovulatory pattern.

An important point to remember is that this method may only be practised if the couple are able to discuss the subject; an impossibility in many homes.

When the man chooses this method, the enforced abstinence is usually borne with a good grace. But when it is the wife who is attempting to enforce it on a reluctant partner (who cannot see what is wrong with another method of his own choosing), then a good deal of nervous tension can result. In both cases, i.e. when the man wants the method and when he does not, he is certainly going to claim his dues when the charts give him the green light. This does away with spontaneity in love-making which can be particularly distressing to those who have, perhaps, already developed a habit of spontaneity. So often in these cases one finds that everything has gone all right until, say, the birth of the sixth child, when the need to practise birth control may suddenly arise. Such people find the method a great strain.

When the husband is often away from home, the atmosphere created by a reunion to the strains of 'Not tonight, dear, I'm fertile' is clearly not one conducive to domestic harmony.

The basic theme of this book is an attempt to show that peace on earth depends on domestic peace, which in turn depends upon sexual harmony. The work of creating sexual harmony in their married lives is the work that women were primarily created to perform. A contraceptive method which relies upon an aggressive imposition of sexual abstinence on the male by the female is clearly as grave an infringement of right order as is the aggressive imposition of male sexuality upon the female. Indeed, the results of feminine anti-sex aggression would be more disastrous than the results we have witnessed hitherto of male sexual aggression. For in the past the woman, in the capacity of mother, was nailed to her role of victim. But when the position is reversed, what is to maintain the loyalty of the man to the marital bond?

If women have borne injustice so long it is because they have had to, for the sake of their children. Men do not have to, and in view of the urgency of the male sexual drive are not likely to.

It should be added here that for those women who have husbands who regard a state of total intoxication every Saturday night as normal the method would be only workable, or safe, if along with the temperature charts and thermometers and menstrual calculators each wife is also provided with a chastity girdle complete with time lock.

For these reasons the author will not advise any woman on this method of birth control, unless and until she can produce evidence that her husband really wants it.

When the man himself makes this method the method of his choice, and his wife has confidence in his sincerity and ability to work it, then it is a good method and one likely to become better as knowledge of the physiological factors involved becomes more complete.

The Male Sheath or Condom

This method of contraception is probably the most popular and widespread at the present time. The necessary articles are easily obtainable at any chemist.

The condom is simply a thin rubber device that rolls over the erect penis and contains it, as a glove-finger does a finger. There is a space at the end for the reception of the seminal fluid, and after use the appliance is disposed of.

The sheath (french letter) is a considerably thicker article, that is not disposed of after use, but washed and retained for further use.

It is commonly believed amongst the young that this method of contraception requires no experience in its handling. This is a mistaken view as many are liable to learn to their cost. Quite apart from the obvious danger of a defect in the rubber such as a tear caused by the finger nail, there remains the danger that it might be applied too late, after there has been genital contact and fluid containing sperm might have escaped. There is also the possibility of the condom slipping off on withdrawal. These matters are easily enough handled with experience, but their hazards are such as to make desirable the concurrent use of a spermicidal pessary.

Reviewing the method under the previous headings one discovers the following:

1. The method depends for its application upon preceding sexual stimulation, and its use therefore does constitute an infringement on the course of the act. Some men find this no drawback at all, others find it an intolerable embarrassment. In the latter case, the attitude of the wife is going to prove decisive, in whether the method is to prove workable. The wife who approaches her husband's embarrassment with kindly encouragement should soon be able to dispel this difficulty.

2. This question depends entirely upon the man's confidence and attitude. Some men say that the rubber interferes with sensation, others say it does not, or not enough to matter.

From the woman's point of view, objections raised would refer to the absence of the sensation evoked by seminal emision, and the resulting absence of seminal fluid in the vagina. To some this would seem an intolerable deprivation, to others the matter is of no interest.

3. Under this head, the use of the condom raises very many and interesting questions. Where this method is chosen by the man and applied by him without reference to his wife's feelings, then on many accounts is wrong done:

(i) Its use can deprive a woman of any say in the matter of conceptions that she might desire. Its imposition in these circumstances is almost as unjust an infringement of female rights as interrupted coitus. [Not as gross, because the possibility of normal sexual satisfaction is still left to her. She is not both sexually tortured *and* deprived of children as she is by withdrawal.]

(ii) At times when the husband is drunk, or very tired, or just plain careless in its use then the method can become a great source of anxiety to the wife.

(iii) The woman is deprived of any beneficial principle that is contained in the seminal fluid, with which by this method she has no contact.

On the other hand, when this method is chosen by the wife, and applied by the wife to her husband, then the method at once takes on a different aspect. Here again, of course, it is very necessary for the woman to consider her husband's feelings. If he does not like the method, for whatever reasons, and cannot be persuaded out of his dislike, then it behoves the wife to think of a different method. The only time when she is justified in making its use conditional upon intercourse taking place at all is when he is insisting upon intercourse and no other method is available. Such a time can well arise in the few weeks following child-birth. At such a time the woman is not likely herself to be wanting intercourse, and other methods are often quite inapplicable. In these circumstances any woman is quite entitled to tell her man that he must use the condom or sleep in another bed.

4. The only side effects that would seem to be of any consequence are those of psychogenic origin, resulting from the kind of difficulties outlined above. This method above all others would seem to call for great tact and kindness in its right handling. Where such mutual consideration is strongly present, it would seem to be a very good method. When these qualities are not present, then it can be truly said that the condom can bring with it all the plagues of hell.

The Vaginal Diaphragm

The principle in this method is the insertion by the woman of a circular rubber appliance with a springy metal rim. When in place this occludes (shuts off) the cervix (or mouth of the womb) from the rest of the vagina, and thus is seminal fluid prevented from entering the higher parts of the female tract. A variation is the cervical cap, which is smaller, of thicker rubber, and simply fits over the mouth of the womb itself.

Both are left in place after intercourse for at least 8 hours, and may be left in for the whole 24 hours and simply removed for washing and reinsertion. In all cases is it most strenuously recommended that the use of the diaphragm or cap be augmented by the application to the appliance of a spermicidal cream, of a kind not detrimental to rubber. This is necessary on account of the possibility of a number of sperm (only one out of the millions present would be sufficient to cause pregnancy) finding their way past the rim of the diaphragm or cap.

These methods require the services of a doctor or nurse, experienced in the work, for the purpose of determining the correct size and shape of appliance for the particular anatomical configuration of the individual woman.

This is the mainstay of the method taught by the Family Planning Association in its clinics throughout the country (though it should be noted that other methods are also taught, if asked for).

Here again, let this method be reviewed under the four headings outlined at the beginning of the chapter:

1. A woman wearing a properly fitting diaphragm should not be conscious of its presence, nor should the man be able to feel it during intercourse. If he can feel it he won't like it. Some men swear they always can detect the presence of a diaphragm, but most would seem to be quite unaware of its presence.

The method is applied by the woman herself, and ideally is done so as a matter of habit, irrespective of whether intercourse is specifically intended, some time previously to the instigation of the act. When used thus, there is no interference with the course of the act itself.

Occasionally, women complain that the rubber interferes with sensation. But many find rather the reverse to be true. The rubber is exceedingly thin (though strong) and light, in the more modern types available now and the accompanying spermicidal cream offers a most welcome form of lubrication.

2. A woman who has confidence in her diaphragm, has complete confidence in it. She has had it fitted and checked by a doctor. She has inserted it herself and knows it to be in place. She is left free to enter into sexual relations without any fear at all. This confidence is rapidly transferred to her partner. Under these circumstances marital intercourse rapidly takes on a new character.

THIS, let us all look now, is THE method that has both instigated and maintained the revolution in woman's status. All honour is due to those manufacturing firms who many many years ago saw birth control as pre-eminently woman's problem, and devoted so much time and thought and energy towards perfecting a technique that would remain easily handled, comfortable, reliable and at all times within the control of the woman herself.

Of all the great works that men have undertaken for women, this must surely rank amongst the noblest. The work was instigated at a time when financial reward was very slight and the risks considerable. It was done in the teeth of social disapproval and in the teeth of great apathy on the part of the medical profession at large. The first men who devised these things at such risk to themselves must one day be named and honoured by all women as 'the instigators of the revolution'.

3. Under this head sufficient has already been said.

4. It is sometimes stated by persons who make it their business to decry contraceptives in all forms that this method 'causes cancer of the womb'. There is no serious evidence to support this. Cancer of the womb is exceedingly common and can just as easily be correlated with multiple pregnancy.

The method does, however, still present several major drawbacks in some cases. First and foremost is the emotional difficulty that some women experience when required to touch their own genitals. Early upbringing has a large part to play in this. It is all part of the 'most forbidden thing'. To overcome this may call for much patience on the part of the doctor. But when it is strongly present it should not be battled with, but left in peace, and another method sought for.

Secondly, the method requires forethought, intelligence and determination on the part of the woman. Where these qualities are lacking, the method is doomed from the outset. To insert a diaphragm only 'when I can remember' is not adequate. To use the same diaphragm long after the rubber has perished or when it has ceased to fit correctly is to court disaster.

Thirdly, there are some women (particularly those who have given birth to a large number of children) whose parts are so battered by their multiple confinements that no appliance can be made to stay in place. Such cases are rare but they do exist.

Lastly, there are those women who simply don't like diaphragms. They don't like the mess, they don't like the personal responsibility. Where they cannot find another method these women must needs ask themselves which they like least, the mess of a diaphragm or the mess of a confinement. The choice is theirs.

Chemical Agents Alone

These are of many types, ranging from gels, tablets, foaming tablets, oil-based pessaries, creams. As can be seen, a lot of ingenuity has been applied to this subject, and virtually every method of medicating the vagina explored.

The use of such agents alone is indicated when a diaphragm cannot be fitted, and where no other method is obtainable or acceptable.

The principle behind their use is twofold, that of supplying a 'barrier' to prevent the passage of sperm into the higher parts of the female tract, and that of destroying the sperms present by their spermicidal action.

An advantage of this type of method for some is that these agents can be obtained direct from the chemist without the necessity of first consulting a doctor.

A disadvantage is that this type of method can only be applied immediately prior to intercourse, and this can be a source of embarrassment and nuisance.

The Pill

This is a revolutionary method in its own right, with no one having more than a few years' experience in its use. So much has recently been written on this subject by others, so much is the interest it has raised. To the advent of this first oral method of contraception must be ascribed the sudden awakening of popular interest in the whole question of birth control.

Whereas in the past any consideration of method had to concentrate on the somewhat embarrassing details of the act, this method and the publicity attached to it have managed to make the whole subject approachable.

The birth pill is actually a tablet, there are many varieties, in the main containing some female hormones in controlled dosages. The commonest one depends upon the woman taking one tablet each day for 20 days (21 days in some cases), of each monthly cycle.

The preparations act on the glands of the body in such a manner as to inhibit ovulation for the whole of each cycle. The hormone they contain is of the same type as that produced by the female glands during pregnancy, in which state it serves a similar purpose, namely, the inhibition of ovulation so that second pregnancy cannot start before the finish of the first.

Examined under the four headings, as done previously with the other methods, one discovers the following:

1. The main attraction of this method is the absence of any appliance, and the fact that there is no need to mess with anything, either before, during or after the act. The act itself takes place in its natural setting with full scope for spontaneity and without any thought or calculation other than that which is required by the woman herself to ensure that the pills have been taken as instructed.

2. The method seems to be extremely reliable and confidence is increasing in it all the time.

3. The whole question of feminine control is admirably answered by this method. Too much so in the opinion of some who feel that responsibility should be shared. This attitude is going to become ever more apparent, as the present generation of young people enter into their marriages with an ever increasing sense of it being a shared enterprise. Those women who have experienced only the old kind, which has total female subjugation as its mainstay, find it difficult to imagine how different a marriage can be. The answer to this objection may well be found in the present development of an oral pill for use by the male. Then each partner can take it in turns to have their hormonal system under fire, as it were.

4. There are no known harmful side effects. Some women find the release from tension and anxiety that is brought by the pill so revolutionary that they stand in need of firm guidance and counsel during the time when the new mental adjustments are being made. At such a time, above all times, does she stand in need of the support of her religious counsellors. The present failure of the Roman Catholic clergy to provide such counsel is one of the most serious blots on the contemporary social scene.

On a less dramatic scale, the kind of changes that are most frequently noted are to do with the feeling of generally increased well-being that the use of the pill so often brings. Women who before have been too anxious to eat or sleep properly start in and do so, with a subsequent increase of weight. Others who drowned their past miseries by overeating and sleeping begin to see in this method a return of hope. They begin to take more interest in their appearance, get out and about more, and generally lose weight and look better for doing so.

The question of long-term side effects awaits clarification, there is no other way of discovering other than by forging ahead and seeing what happens. The first man to sail around the world didn't do so by sitting at home worrying as to whether he would come back alive.

On the other hand, there is no reason why, wherever possible, this method should not be alternated every one to two years, with another for a similar duration. It is difficult to see how the pill, used in this way, could prove any different in its long-term effects than that which results from the hormonal upheaval caused by repeated pregnancy.

When all is said and done the greatest blessing this pill brings is to offer a way 'in' for women who might otherwise never find one. When the situation is desperate, few women will find they CAN'T swallow a pill. The same women might genuinely prefer to be put to death in public rather than insert a diaphragm, or even consent to the presence of a condom in the house. But a pill they can swallow. Once having embarked on this course their attitudes rapidly undergo a change. This in turn influences their husband's thinking. A domestic situation that one year previously might have appeared insoluble is found, to the astonishment of all concerned, to have taken on an altogether different aspect. A breathing space has been afforded in which the couple have been relieved of the destructive effects of the pressure of anxieties too big to be borne. Such a breathing space affords the partners the possibility of discussing the problem together in a calmer frame of mind. From such a discussion might emerge a different solution, acceptable to both.

One of the problems raised by the pill, which might well be discussed here, is that which it raises for the family doctor himself. He is the usual person asked for these prescriptions. Under the terms of the National Health Service, this is not strictly 'treatment', so he is not obliged to give it. The time and thought required to give a prescription (a private one) are considerable. He may not claim remuneration, neither from the National Health Service nor from the patient, for this service. At the moment this service is either performed through motives of pure altruism, or else from the fear that if it is withheld the patient may take her card elsewhere. This is not a satisfactory state of affairs, and does not lead to the most favourable atmosphere for the consideration of the associated problems.

There is no reason why women should not pay for professional advice in this matter, and if they were required to do so it would encourage general practitioners to take more interest in the whole business. Another possibility is to make the giving of advice about the pill part of the local authority service, for which people would still have to pay. The Family Planning Association itself does a lot of this work, but it is doubtful whether their facilities are adequate to cope with the ever increasing rush of demands for these prescriptions. The family doctor is bearing the brunt of this work and he is already over-worked. A solution along altogether different lines is awaiting discovery. It will not emerge until a crisis develops. It is becoming increasingly obvious to the author, from her ex-perience as locum tenens for many general practitioners, that a crisis is developing. What is happening is that people who have obtained contraceptive knowledge from chemists (who in-cidentally, have for years borne the brunt of this work, without any remuneration whatsoever), or from anxious whisperings in dark corners, are now learning that all they need do is to go to the doctor, ask for 'the pill', and, hey presto, that's it. For every woman who comes home with her prescription today (for which she has to pay 10/– a month at the moment, though many firms are starting to bring their prices down considerably) there will be another five at the surgery door next month. Having myself coped with winter evening surgeries of over fifty in number, I frankly tremble for my colleagues in general practice who are going to have to find time to advise women on the problems of the pill within that setting. Small wonder that many doctors are 'concerned' about the pill. If the author was in full time general practice, she would hesitate to have anything to do with it.

A consideration of present methods of family limitation would not be complete without adding a word on sterilisation and abortion.

As far as this country is concerned, these expediencies cannot strictly be called methods at all. They are blunderbuss tactics resorted to when matters have already got out of hand. Both these methods are to be found incorporated into the official policy of other countries who have a population problem very different from our own. In India programmes of sterilisation of men are under way and in Japan abortion, as a method, has been officially encouraged. It is not felt by the author that any comment by anyone in this country on such methods is in place. We do not live in India, and know nothing of the realities with which they are contending. Let us rather first put our own house in order, and then perhaps we will be in a better position to help others find more constructive solutions.

As far as this country is concerned, two remarks can be made at the outset, which apply equally to both expediencies.

1. In the case of both female sterilisation and abortion, an abdominal operation is required. This means a major operation, one which, in the author's experience, gynaecologists are extremely loth to undertake. Their basic attitude seems to be one of irritation that things should ever have been allowed to get to such a pass. They are only ever undertaken when the circumstances are of a peculiarly difficult nature, and the medical indications very clearly expressible. This consideration alone precludes a discussion of these things as 'methods'. In this country, they simply are not.

The fact that many married people do in fact contravene the law and seek abortion from non-medical sources merely serves to emphasise their need for help and education in a more constructive approach.

2. When things do in fact reach this pass, it will commonly be discovered that the woman has been the uncomplaining victim, for years, of ill-treatment by her husband, or medical apathy, or spiritual terror. Sometimes all these factors are present at once and have been allowed to operate with merciless efficiency until the point is reached when someone in authority, possibly no one less than the woman herself, realises that something must be done and that something will have to be very fundamental.

As far as natural law arguments go, it has already been pointed out that women themselves have a nature. Where this nature has been pitiably abused, then it is liable to take its own revenge.

Summary

From all that has been said, it is clear what a highly indi-
vidualistic matter the choice of contraceptive becomes for those
married people who wish to limit the size of their family.
However, two principles do emerge which can be stressed in
summary.

1. It is necessary for both partners to exercise the maximum
consideration for the feelings of the other, in making a choice
as to method.

2. When such consideration is absent in the male approach,
and plain arrogance takes over by force, then the woman has
the right to resort to subterfuge. For this is HER problem. And
this applies as much to achieving a desired pregnancy, as in
avoiding an undesired one.

In attempting to create a happy home, a man and woman
are doing the greatest work that can be done anywhere by
anyone, and God will bless their efforts and help them mightily
to achieve this worthy aim.

It has been found again and again that a practice that is
instigated in circumstances of personal terror may still blossom
and bear fruit in a new kind of existence. An existence in which
the appearance of another child might come to be recognised
as the greatest of all blessings.

A new kind of attitude to sex means a new kind of marital
experience, and this means a new kind of attitude to our
children.

PART THREE

A SUMMARY

WE hear, everywhere, common folk, guided by their own common sense, asserting that the love between man and woman can and should be expressed in terms of sexual union. The popular songs of the day assert this dictum with robust and ear-splitting assurance. Nor is it only the young who appreciate these songs. Many of an older generation enjoy them, recognising, perhaps, some strains of a universal truth. And in this, of course, they are quite right.

We all know that the love of which these songs sing is the greatest thing in the world. A man falls in love and this event, 'like a certain divine rage and enthusiasm . . . works a revolution in his mind and body; unites him to his race, pledges him to the domestic and civic relations, carries him with a new sympathy into nature, enhances the power of the senses, opens the imagination, adds to his character heroic and sacred attributes, establishes marriage and gives permanence to human society' (R. W. Emerson: Essays, *Love*).

Or, in the more popular idiom: 'With a love like that, you know you should be glad.' And, of course, we are glad.

Against this, what are we to say of a religious influence that tends to foster mistrust of such an all-embracing drive towards the great and the good?

Here we are on slippery ground again, for is it not religious influence itself that assures us stability in the assertion that love will be unto death?

Life is long, and love does not always last.

In the meantime there are the children to be fed.

In remaining loyal to our own highest aspirations there is no human being who does not stand in need of guidance; and friends are not always there to give it.

One of the purposes of religion is to supply it, to supply that leading light to the soul that will guide the individual through all the crises and difficulties of life, to his anchorage in heaven, which is his true resting place.

Few are any longer interested in a heaven 'up there'. All are hungering for the 'living bread that came down from heaven'. We want our heaven here on earth, and why should we not? Have we not all been taught to pray: 'Thy Kingdom come; Thy will be done on Earth, as it is in Heaven'? To build the kingdom of heaven here on earth is the ideal that captivates the hearts of all men of good will everywhere.

Those who have been brought up in the Christian tradition are entitled to look to the Christian religion for this guiding light. That there is a great upsurging of interest in the Christian religion is plain. How the leaders of other denominations are meeting this challenge to their spiritual resources is not my concern. As a Roman Catholic, I am interested in one thing only, and that is what my own religion has to offer. It has been shown how the official line of the Roman Catholic Church is at the moment failing to supply a guiding light to its adherents; is indeed doing worse and actually guiding them on to the rocks. But it is my contention that this failure is a failure of men and of the legal system they are chained to, and does not in fact represent an inadequacy in the mystical content of Roman Catholic doctrine. Let this content be understood aright and applied aright, and Roman Catholic theology is eminently able to find, from within itself, a solution to the present impasse.

My understanding of these matters, as I will explain, constitutes the reason why, far from leaving the Roman Catholic Church, I would have everyone inside. But first must come the revolution. This revolution is not to be worked from without by violence, but from within by the gradual triumph of that Spirit that has already passed judgement: 'Woe unto you lawyers who lay men with burdens grievous to be born, burdens that you do not touch yourselves with as much as one of your little fingers.'

The power of these lawyers will be overthrown just as soon as those in the Roman Catholic Church who recognise the evil they do find the spiritual energy to give battle. Before such strength can be summoned, such people need to see clearly, and for themselves, what it is they are going to set up in place of the old order.

To this end the following reflections are offered. These matters reflect my spiritual insight, as I understand it. They are simply the answer to the question: 'How do you justify remaining in the Roman Catholic Church, and with what do you propose to replace the old order?' Or, to put the question in its most telling form: 'What do you propose to teach your children?'

THEOLOGICAL REFLECTIONS

If I am asked why, as a doctor, I feel I must put my fingers into theological pies instead of concentrating on medicine and leaving theology to the theologians, I answer that it is because I am also a Roman Catholic who understands the dilemma of the theologians and has at the same time a personal interest in the vindication of Roman Catholic theology.

Having contended myself with the problem of birth control as a Roman Catholic, I know that it is a question that a Catholic can scarcely bend on without breaking. The fact that some have achieved the ability to bend is because they have assumed that the theologians in Rome are going to do something about the situation at an early date. I do not think they can do anything without in fact 'breaking' first. So break they must, and their (the theologians') problem is going to be that of gathering together the pieces. But that comes later. In the meantime every other possibility, other than apparent total collapse, must be explored by them. It must be remembered that the force of public opinion itself cannot ever be sufficient, on its own, to alter the Pope's thinking, or that of any of the bishops, any more than their opinion is doing anything to alter the thinking of the world in their favour. The impasse is real and the crisis is mounting.

A change in official teaching, a change that is so desperately needed, cannot and will not come until the theologians of the Roman Catholic Church come to understand that it is the Almighty Himself who is now pleading with them through the cries of distress of their own people. But even when they do come to realise this (and they seem a long way from it yet), they will still have the problem of 'squaring' the official 'about turn' with all their past thinking on this subject.

This happens to be a problem that I have myself faced and overcome to my own satisfaction, and therefore my contribution may well be of value to other Roman Catholics in the same difficulties, be they bishops or housewives.

The dilemma presented by the violence of the sexual drive, in an already over-populated environment, is a dilemma one can comfortably think about in an armchair UNTIL it strikes home. When it strikes, it strikes with the violence of a hurricane. This hurricane is now about to strike our bishops, as it struck me just over two years ago. I am at least two years ahead of the bishops, and I know what it is they are going through, and still have to go through. If I can help anyone with these reflections of mine then I am only too glad to do so, and it will help me to come to terms with the unspeakable bitterness and suffering I have myself endured on this matter, and every single member of the Roman Catholic priesthood must yet endure.

I find that there are more Roman Catholics coming to my clinic asking me how to maintain their faith than to learn methods of birth control. It is also clear, from the letters I have received, some of which have appeared in this book, that many Roman Catholics have already faced and overcome the specifically medical problems associated with their need to practise contraception. Family Planning Association clinics, family doctors, generously minded pharmacists and pharmaceutical firms have all combined to propagate contraceptive knowledge. But from none of these sources can a Roman Catholic obtain knowledge that will help him maintain his spiritual stability. Their marriages, their homes, indeed their very lives have been and are being saved, but in the process it seems to some that their souls are being lost.

People come to see me, to ask me about myself and to try to obtain some of the assurance they believe that I have. There is nothing for it but to set to and go over all the groundwork of my own spiritual life. I am required to delve deeply into my own spiritual reading and explain at length the terms in which I see this problem in relation to the Roman Catholic Church.

This is time-consuming indeed, and it seems to me that it might prove helpful, both to myself and to those who cannot travel far to see me, if I were to put into writing some of these thoughts on spiritual matters.

So in this third part of this book I *do* delve into mysticism, theology and Church history. On none of these subjects am I a great scholar, I merely have done a certain amount of reading and gleaned a certain number of ideas. So none of these ideas are in themselves original, I have obtained them all from Roman Catholic scholars. Any originality they might appear to have is due entirely to the sifting process of my own mind and the order I have chosen to present them in. Roman Catholic theology is so vast, and her doctors and mystics so holy and so numerous, that by no means should anyone allow himself to feel cramped or limited by me.

So true is this that I would have in every parish a clinic like mine where doctors can prescribe the contraceptives their patients need and priests, who feel drawn to this sort of work, can dispense their own Catholic insight into the associated spiritual problems.

The need exists in all our parishes now. To wait for a green light from Rome would be to wait too long. The Pope and the bishops in Rome have their own problems in relation to this matter, and they are very great problems indeed. They should not be stampeded into finding a solution, the finding of which might well take years. There are many and extraordinary facts of confusion and disharmony awaiting manifestation, as far as Rome is concerned. So let it be. Let not the faith of the individual Roman Catholic be disturbed.

The idea of a united christendom with a visible head in Rome, in direct historical line with Jesus Christ, is too great an idea to abandon casually. Let those whose destiny it is to bring this idea to its full realisation be allowed to labour to this end without distraction, and let us, the ordinary folk of the Church, set to and apply our own Catholic principles to the problems we find on our doorsteps.

That is how I have proceeded myself and I see no reason why others should not follow my example, including priests.

The bishops are going to be far too busy to stop them, and anyway, where a priest finds his own mind made up who CAN stop him? If he knows he is right, he can take consolation from the thought that the law of this land is in his favour. If the bishop should order him to stop, he can do as I did and ignore the unreasonable command. If legal action is threatened against him, let him stand fast. This is a free country, he will be astonished at HOW free it is when he once has the courage to put the matter to the test. This is not Nazi Germany, even though sometimes the bishops behave as though they think it is.

He will find the people of England on his side, Catholics and non-Catholics, and he will find all the saints of heaven fighting for him.

Provided he holds fast to his Catholic faith, says Mass, serves his people's spiritual needs and gives his bishop his due, then nothing can stop him from serving God in this way.

I am not putting this line of conduct forward as the ideal in all times and places. Clearly, authority itself ought not to be flouted in this way. But the times are extraordinary; authority has lost its way, and until it rediscovers itself once more, ordinary people must carry on in spite of it, after all, we expected the Germans to do so under Hitler.

For, as I have said already, this matter has come as Judgement Day itself to our Church. Our Lord will not enquire of any of us regarding the laws of the Church that we have kept or failed to keep to the letter. He will judge us according to just one yardstick, and that is how we have treated 'the least of these His brethren'.

Ultimately, when the bishops have got themselves sorted out and the Church reorganised along more realistic lines, they will be very grateful to the 'rebel' priests, who will have got this work of mercy under way, and will have already started to vindicate the reputation of their Church, a reputation that the bishops will have brought to a very low ebb indeed by the time they have made up their minds on this and associated problems.

I have shown that this kind of thing CAN be done, and particularly can it be done in England. Then gradually will the faithful of other countries come to copy what England will have initiated. Thus will the Roman Catholic Church be reformed from within.

The particular subjects that I chose to write about here concern:

1. The mystical doctrines of St. John of the Cross, which are particularly applicable to the spiritual needs of a Roman Catholic people in a state of open conflict with their spiritual superiors, for in such a state of bitter spiritual conflict were all the works of St. John of the Cross first conceived.

2. The Dogma of the Co-redemptrix, the still undefined content of which has supplied me with that particular 'certainty' that so many Catholics envy me for possessing. And lastly,

3. The medieval concept of law, which has been swept away by all the flotsam of the Renaissance, and in which are to be found the true principles of justice and individual freedom.

The dictum 'The will of the Emperor has the force of law' is a dictum of the Renaissance, and it is upon the Roman civil code, that made this dictum its own, that the canon law of the Roman Catholic Church is based.

Until that time a very different state of affairs prevailed in the Catholic Church. It is to the Middle Ages that we must now return.

CHAPTER XIII

THE CONTRIBUTION FROM MYSTICISM

ONE of the greatest of all Christian mystical authors was St. John of the Cross, a sixteenth-century Spanish Carmelite friar. So dangerously revolutionary was his doctrine considered by his Carmelite brothers, whose way of life he wished to reform, that they took him prisoner and all but murdered him, by starvation, solitary confinement and bi-weekly floggings. Their justification was that he was mad and this was the right treatment for madness. After nine months he managed to escape from their hands, and contrived to live the rest of his life within his own reformed order and write poetry and mystical works of unsurpassed power and beauty. In the course of time the Roman Catholic Church canonised him, and gave hime the title of 'Doctor of the Universal Church'.

But for all that, his influence has remained all but negligible outside his own order; until, that is, an Anglican, Professor Allison Peers, translated his works into English. Thanks to his labours, and by no means thanks to the official Voice of our pastors, have English-speaking Catholics been able to benefit from the sanity and humanity of this truly marvellous visionary. The 'official' view of him remains what it was in his day, i.e. 'a very dangerous author, very unsettling in his effects'. They dress this verdict up slightly, as they have to, in view of his titles, and stress rather that he is only suitable for the *very* spiritually advanced. What they mean is that they have not themselves advanced sufficiently to understand the meaning of the first words he wrote.

It is hoped that what is written here will help to that understanding, which is better arrived at late than never.

The basic teaching of St. John of the Cross centred around 'The Dark Night', as the key to all spiritual advance. The meaning of the Dark Night is this: every soul in its natural state, enjoys the light of natural day. Information from our senses tells us things about the world we live in. Our higher faculties of memory, reasoning power, and ability to choose, sort out this material and supply us with a knowledge of reality that is natural knowledge. This knowledge is the knowledge of this world, is the daylight of this world and it is good. But it is man's destiny to attain to supernatural knowledge, and to a good that transcends the good of this world, to nothing less than a sharing of God's life on terms of equality with his creator. To become fitted for this life the soul must become familiar with heavenly things, so that it can live in the light of heavenly day. There are thus two 'days', the daylight of this world and the daylight of heaven. These two days are separated by night. To attain the supernatural knowledge, which is the daylight of heaven, the soul must traverse this night. Before a soul is moved to set out on this journey, and leave behind it the comfortable certainties of this world, it first must be inspired to do so, by having been allowed to catch a glimpse of the splendour of the supernatural light.

This light comes from God who is the source of all light and just a glimpse of this light has the effect of blinding the soul. Just as the eyes are temporarily blinded by looking at the sun, so is the soul blinded by the light that comes from heaven. Blinded to the point of total spiritual darkness. Souls who have caught a glimpse of this heavenly light cannot live any more by the light of natural day but, blinded as they are, must needs move forward towards the source of supernatural knowledge, which means moving steadily and relentlessly forward into a darkness that is ever darker. This is 'The dark night of the soul' about which St. John of the Cross wrote volumes. These volumes were written with a view to guiding the soul through this night. They explain all the subjective sensations of spiritual darkness and their meaning.

A study of these works would give a clue to many modern psychiatrists and priests who are baffled by the spiritual agony of their patients and penitents: an agony that cannot be comprehended in medical terms. For this is the agony of spiritual advance. So well did St. John of the Cross understand this that he made such darkness and such agony an absolute prerequisite of any spiritual advance. Because of this, he loved this night, and sang of the splendours of its darkness, and would have it ever darker and darker. For in this darkness is the soul purified and prepared for the light of the new day, which is union with God, the soul's true spouse.

He compares this journey in darkness to the tryst that a lover keeps, who climbs the secret stairs to the chamber of his beloved, a journey that is 'lit only by heart's inmost fire ablaze'. The journey itself as thrilling in its implications as any journey could possibly be. 'Oh Night that guided me, Oh night more lovely than the dawn.'

With an approach such as this to spiritual problems, who would be afraid to leave behind him the old and comfortable certainties?

'God is as dark night to the soul' was his dictum, and to find God we must turn our back on every image we have made of Him, and reject every preconceived idea that we might have of Him, and seek him in darkness, where we shall certainly find Him. Oh, that more of our priests might study this author!

It has already been pointed out how Roman Catholics as a religious group have hitherto enjoyed a great sense of certainty in their religion, with their infallible Pope and their cut-and-dried morality, and how suddenly are they now precipitated into darkness, by the failure of their leaders to understand their needs in a world that is changing faster than they can keep track of it. This darkness has been likened to an eclipse of the sun in this book. For Catholics understand the teaching voice of the Church to be the voice of God. This guidance has shone for them as the sun has shone in the sky. Now this light has become darkness, a darkness as inpenetrable as night.

According to the dictum of St. John of the Cross, this experience should be welcomed as a sign of great portent.

CHAPTER XIV

THE CONTRIBUTION FROM DOGMA

REFERENCE has already been made to a new dogma for the delivery of which the Catholic Church must now go into labour. What is this dogma, what is its theological background and what is its bearing on the Roman Catholic situation generally and the birth control controversy in particular?

The new dogma is that of the Co-redemptrix. The development of Mariology within the Roman Catholic Church requires this final definition for its completion.

The fact that Catholic theologians might appear to be keeping off Mariology is due to expediency. It has become fashionable to think first of the reunion of Christians and the need not to upset the 'separated brethren'. The reunion is sometimes seen as an 'all boys together' kind of tea party, a concept that is utterly repudiated by the author, who is convinced that the divisions in christendom have by no means arisen by chance, but represent historical developments of a truth that has itself become fragmented. The originators of the Protestant revolt and every reformed sect that developed thereafter were all protesting against something real and reforming themselves according to real Christian concepts. Thus every Christian sect has its origins in truth, and it is to these origins that every sect should now return. Christ is the Truth and Christ desires unity, but this will not come by straining after it as an end in itself. It is something that Christ will Himself grant to those who seek Him for His *own* sake. Where is Christ to be found? He has told us that He is not to be found in this place or in that place, but in the secret places of the soul. Access to these places can only come about by a fervent dedication to personal religious integrity.

As far as the Roman Catholic Church goes that must mean that she must here and now forget 'the separated brethren' and seek her own integrity along the lines of that bent of theological development that is already pre-eminently her own.

When the Roman Catholic Church has come face to face with her own truth, and wooed it and embraced it and made it all glorious and all her own, then will she be in a position to look the separated brethren in the face. Whether they will like what they see remains to be discovered, but that is their business. Our business is exclusively that of seeing that our Church becomes more and more that which she has been called upon by God to be.

To all the separated brethren who gaze with puzzled anxiety at Roman Catholic Marian theology I would say 'Let no man deceive you – We do not teach the same doctrine about the redemption as is taught by any other Christian sect. We teach a doctrine that is peculiarly our own, and this doctrine is dependent upon an 'insight' into the Virgin Mary and her role in the scheme of salvation, that is NOT to be found in scripture, but is part of our very experience of the Christian religion. An experience that has its counterpart in no other sect.'

The Roman Catholic interest in the Virgin Mary is NOT an accident and it has manifested itself throughout history in the definition of dogmas relating to her. The dogma of the Immaculate Conception and the dogma of the Assumption are not just fancy ways of saying what the whole rest of the Christian world takes for granted. Very far from it. They are declarations of Roman Catholic truth that have their counterpart in nothing else whatever.

Before the old order can be swept away and the new Church of the new Christian era born, the historic mission of the old order must first be fulfilled. As far as the Roman Catholic Church goes this means that the last Marian dogma must be defined. This is the dogma of the Co-redemptrix, the content of which is implied in all Roman Catholic theology.

It is not for me to define this dogma, that is the work of theologians. All that need be said here is that this dogma is giving to the woman, the mother of Christ, a status in the scheme of salvation equal to that of her son.

We say of Mary that the Holy Ghost was so enamoured of her spiritual beauty that He took her to Himself, and the issue of that union was Christ.

It was said of Christ, by the priests of the Church of His day, that as everyone knew where He came from He could not be

Christ; 'For when Christ cometh, no man knows whence He comes, and this man, we all know whence He comes.' It would seem that they expected Him to materialise out of thin air. That He should have been born of a woman and reared by a woman and given to the world by a woman would constitute a disproof of His claim. Christ's work of redemption cannot be separated from the work of His mother, who under the providence of God literally made Christ's advent possible, and translated it from a prophecy to a reality, by her willingness to fulfil the destiny that had been laid upon her.

It is suggested that the pivotal point of Mary's spiritual life – the act of her will that gave her the status of co-redeemer with her son – was the moment when she consented to pregnancy. To understand the magnitude of this decision in its real-life context, as distinct from its theological implications, it must be remembered that when the matter was put to her she was not married but espoused. To become pregnant other than by sexual intercourse with her espoused would lay her open to the charge of adultery, for which the penalty was death by stoning. Having consented to this pregnancy at the hands of the Holy Ghost (and here 'consent' means to willingly accept a pre-ordained fate, to make the best of it) she could hardly rely upon her own resources to convince her espoused that she was still a virgin. Such a proposition is self-contradictory, and would have met with no greater credence in her day than in our own. Yet into this situation of total misunderstanding by her contemporaries did she willingly precipitate herself just as soon as she realised what was required of her. She did not say that no one would believe her and that she would be surely stoned, but 'Be it done unto me according to thy word'. She was not to know how the Almighty was going to still the anger and jealousy of her espoused, she was content to believe that somehow or other it would be done.

From then on her state of virginity in her married life can only reflect an attitude on the part of her husband. In this matter there can be no 'Credit' attached to her. She remained a virgin (according to Roman Catholic doctrine) BECAUSE her husband made no claim upon her. So in the matter of the conduct of her marital relationship it is clear that she has no specific message to give her spiritual children, for her marriage was unique. There is only one mother of Christ, and the circumstances of her historical motherhood are not likely to be repeated. Therefore, from these physical circumstances, no conclusions applicable to others can be drawn. But from her willingness to launch forth into a spiritual adventure of the first magnitude there are many conclusions to be drawn.

Before listing these, let us remember that the 'Protestant' view of the virgin birth states that Mary was simply chosen, as any other woman might have been chosen, to be Christ's mother, that she was but a passive instrument and had no personal say. The dogmatic assertion of the Roman Catholic Church, which claims an 'inside' knowledge of the facts, is that this was not the case, that she was a 'special' woman BECAUSE she rose to the spiritual challenge of her destiny in a special way. To the question 'What was so special?', there is no answer, other than the one derived from personal contact with her, and this answer must therefore appear in the dogmatic context.

To get back to the spiritual conclusions to be drawn from the fact of Mary's co-operation with the scheme of redemption, the following can be listed:

   (i) The Almighty can and does ask the most extraordinary things of His servants.
  (ii) The most momentous decisions are those made in total spiritual solitude, with reference to no other human being.
 (iii) The effects of these decisions can, and usually do, run directly counter to the established and orthodox view – in her case the view that virgins DO NOT conceive.
 (iv) Given a spiritual generosity equal to hers then the outcome of a single decision can have consequences that can shake the world to its foundations.

These things apply to each and every one of us and are some of the lessons to be learned from Mary.

If the redemption of mankind was achieved on the cross, so was that redemption achieved by Mary, when by her consent to her pregnancy and all that would follow therefrom she made the Crucifixion possible by bringing into the world He who took the Cross to Himself.

That then is an example of the kind of thinking that runs through the mind of a Roman Catholic who believes implicitly in Mary's positive share in the work of the redemption.

The major point that is being made here, in connection with what is written on 'Eve', 'the Second Eve' and 'the Woman', depends for its understanding on the realisation that the advent of oral contraception appears to me to be an event of as great a significance for mankind as was the expulsion from the Garden of Eden.

On that day, the day in which the action of the wife, Eve, led to the disgrace of herself and her husband Adam, mankind entered an era in which all the personal troubles promised by God have been fulfilled with relentless exactitude.

The contraceptive pill has come to woman, as a heavenly reprieve from that primordial doom. It is my contention that this must be willed by God, and I say that the appearance of these drugs can be taken as a sign of God's final pardon to Eve.

It is taught that nothing can happen that is not God's will. Advances that are made in the fields of scientific research are dependent on two factors: 1. The steady pursuit of knowledge on man's part. 2. The willingness on God's part to draw aside the veil of natural knowledge and allow the enquiring mind a glimpse into nature's unknown.

In the case of, say, cancer research, very little progress has been made, in spite of the most prodigious efforts. It would seem that until the moment comes when God, in His infinite goodness, sees that it is good for His children to have a new knowledge, no effort on their part alone will give them the desired result.

It is my belief that the sudden recent spectacular advance in contraceptive knowledge is *a sign from heaven*, and a sign that implies three things:

(i) That Eve is now truly forgiven.
(ii) This necessarily means that we must be on the threshold of a new dispensation, as regards God's dealings with His people, none other than that prophesied in the Apocalypse of St. John the Apostle.
(iii) That this reprieve for the daughters of Eve was won for them by 'the Second Eve', Mary, the mother of

Christ, in whom the Almighty started His work of re-creation, and by whose co-operation in this work the redemption of the human race was secured.

Mary's obedience preceded that of her Son's in time, just as Eve's disobedience had preceded Adam's. It has taken mankind all but 2000 years to digest the meaning of these events, and until they were understood God did not think it good for women to benefit in too revolutionary a sense from the fact of the redemption.

The improvement in woman's lot has come about very gradually indeed, and reflects the time it has taken men to realise that she has in fact been redeemed at all. Now suddenly, the most spectacular and revolutionary improvement imaginable is here within her grasp. That this event should be understood aright, then Mary's role in the scheme of salvation must be understood aright. For in supernatural significance these two matters are as two sides of the one coin.

What all this means *exactly* and the proper mode of its expression is a matter to be left to the experts. But it is a work they should take in hand at once, so that non-Catholics who seek reunion with Rome are enabled to see precisely the nature of the theological climate into which they would be moving.

This must take precedence in importance to any debate on birth control. For this is fundamental. When this theological issue is faced and clarified in its fundamental theological terms, then the matter of birth control will be seen in its proper perspective.

For through the clarification of this dogma will certain matters emerge with crystal clearness; namely the supreme spiritual dignity of 'The Woman' and her freedom to act in her prevailing circumstances, as the Holy Ghost inspires her to act.

Until recent times the Christian world has been all but blinded by the light emanating from Christ, Who is as it were the sun itself, the source of all light, blinded to the light of the moon, which though it can only reflect the sun's light is still a source of heavenly light to the earth, and is as important to the right ordering of life on this earth as is the sun in his way.

In this context, the Virgin Mary represents the moon. In the course of an eclipse, the moon shows her power over the sun, as far as this earth is concerned, for she can darken the sun as nothing else in our experience can.

Thus, it would seem, is the Virgin Mary acting now within the Roman Catholic Church. The issue of the spiritual dignity of women is pre-eminently *her* issue, to make this plain is she now causing the current supernatural eclipse, and the resulting spiritual darkness in the Roman Catholic Church. By the time this darkness lifts men will have come to learn that this moon does indeed have power; they will despise her no longer but give her the honour that is her due. Thus it is through a knowledge of the Virgin Mary that Roman Catholic men will learn to honour all women, and bring the days of their neglect to end.

Who can doubt that woman restored to her original position of dignity in her own and in man's eyes will bring to pass the creation of those conditions on earth that are described in the apocalypse of St. John. That holy city which is the new Jerusalem and is to be sent down all clothed in readiness, like a bride to meet her husband? What else can this be but the Kingdom of God on earth, and who more able to build it than women delivered from spiritual subservience to men and made their true equals in supernatural dignity?

CHAPTER XV

THE CONTRIBUTION FROM HISTORY

REFERENCE has been made continually throughout this book to the 'inadequacy of canon law', to 'an outdated legal system' to 'the chains of a spiritual totalitarianism'. In Part Two, chapter x, p. 100, was given an example of the kind of chains that bind a priest to a particular line of thought. Now it is time to look a little closer and see what it is I am driving at. At this point I would once again stress that I am not in any way an authority on law and its origins; the matters I refer to here are simply matters that have come to my attention and I offer them as a 'clue' which might be followed up with advantage when it comes to re-thinking the whole question of Church organisation.

The whole bent of modern Roman Catholic spirituality is that which makes of passive obedience the cardinal virtue. When a conflict arises between conscience and authority, the 'good' Catholic is one who tramples conscience underfoot and follows authority blindly. This is not how the matter is 'officially' presented because, officially, a well instructed Catholic cannot have a conscience opposed to the Church, because the Church knows only too well that conscience is the voice of God in the soul. And as the Church's teaching is supposed to be the voice of God, how can God speak against Himself? Clearly He cannot. It is obviously easier to treat the protesting conscience as no more than an erroneous 'opinion', rather than to admit the possibility that in any given matter the Church could possibly be mistaken.

So as things stand at the moment, a Catholic with a protesting conscience is either charged with being 'opinionated' and therefore a suitable subject for chastisement, or else with being 'touched' in the head. This last can present a particularly dangerous situation for a priest, and one that he must watch closely, if conscience brings him into conflict with other priests.

That priests can and, I suspect, *do* use a method of 'psychiatric terror' against their more troublesome colleagues is a possibility that I wish the general public to take note of now. When Roman Catholic priests, particularly those known to be of a more independent turn of mind, suddenly are pronounced 'ill' by their superiors, and removed elsewhere, it behoves all who have the cause of the liberty of the individual at heart to take note of what is happening. (For it is my opinion that Catholic priests both can be, and have been, silenced in this way.)

Such a method of spiritual terror can only operate where public opinion is not alerted to the possibilities.

Whether the method used is the one outlined above or simply consists of the kind of spiritual intimidation that has been employed against me, the fact remains that conscience itself cannot get a hearing in our Church today.

It is not that the Catholic Church does not know the difference between conscience and opinion, it is simply that for her present spiritual system to work there is no room for conscience. This is spiritual totalitarianism.

This implicit acceptance of authority, known as passive obedience, is a doctrine that has its roots in the Renaissance and makes the decisive distinction between the Middle Ages and the modern world. The Renaissance was essentially a secular movement inspired in its political conceptions by the precepts of the Roman civil law, as obtained not from the law of the Roman people but drawn up in the eastern empire on principles that we would call dictatorial, by which the will of the Emperor has the force of law.*

Before the Renaissance, the guiding principle of medieval law was the absolute integrity of the individual conscience in relationship to God. Rulers were believed to have been instituted for the sake of peoples, not peoples for the sake of rulers. The power of a ruler was not absolute but limited by appointed bounds. The doctrine of unconditional obedience was foreign to the Middle Ages, for then was every duty of obedience conditioned by the rightness of command!

All authority was therefore bounded by limits established in

* Pope Boniface VIII in 1298 started the Pope-versus-King conflict by his assertion that the law proceeded from his own bosom. It was to this claim that Wycliffe objected. Later, Richard II of England made the same claim for himself.

law. This law was not the will of the ruler, but was established
by custom and developed by reason which commanded the
consent of those who were subject to the law. The great
conception of law and of a free social order based on Christian
ideology was shattered in the Renaissance by the reception of
Roman civil law, and was left only as a tradition that has
now become an aspiration.

The reception of Roman civil law depended largely on
political causes. By subordinating the legal system to the idea
of the state towering over the individual, the path was cleared
for ambitious emperors, grasping princes and lastly, but not
least, the clerical representatives of clerical law and order.

The first forces to tread the road that leads away from the
Middle Ages are the champions of papal absolutism, and it
was this road that led to the break-up of united christendom,
in the Reformation. The doctrine was challenged by the
French revolution and its doctrine of political democracy. But
the very challengers ended up by embracing the same doctrine,
that of the *will of the supreme authority having the force of law*.

In this climate the conscience of the individual in relationship
to God is smothered.

With our experience of Stalinist Russia, and Hitlerite
Germany, clearly the relationship of authority with conscience
requires to be formulated. In this issue the Christian ideology
of the Middle Ages can provide a guide. There authority was
not confused with power, nor was conscience confused with
opinion. Medieval thought denied the right to any man to
subject a fellow man to his will by virtue of economic or social
position. The equal integrity of men in relationship to God was
a cardinal principle of medieval thought, so that no man could
be subjected to the will of another, but must be free to follow
his own conscience in his relationship to God. As however the
existence of human society depends upon order, the support
and maintenance of that order was an equally cardinal condition. It was to solve this apparent contradiction of the authority
of the community with the integrity of the individual that
medieval political thought was directed. The solution was
simply that every right carried with it a corresponding duty,
and the exercise of the right of authority was subject to the
fulfilment of a corresponding duty. Thus was the social fellow-

ship established in law of the rights and duties of parents and children, of landlords and tenants, of masters and servants, and, above all, of rulers and subjects. In all these relationships the absolute integrity of the individual conscience in relationship to God was recognised as supreme.

Roman canon law was drawn up at the time of the Renaissance and was based on precepts drawn from the Roman civil code, which run directly counter to the whole of medieval thought.

The greatest single lesson we have to learn from the time that has elapsed since the Middle Ages is that arbitrary power is the root of all evil. We have seen in our own day this evil blossom forth its hideous fruits in Nazism and Stalinism. We are now coming to see for ourselves the real evil of Spiritual Absolutism that depends for its workings on the same principle, the principle that states that the will of the supreme authority has the force of law. The contrary thesis that belongs to the Roman Catholic Church just AS truly, for it is part of her very foundations in the Middle Ages, is that the *conscience of the individual has the force of law.*

To counteract the spiritual absolutism of our Church, there is only one course of action open, and it is open to every single Roman Catholic whoever he is and wherever he is and that is to recognise the force of conscience where it challenges any of the precepts of autocratic authority claimed by the supreme head of the Church or of the hierarchy.

Conscience is recognised by the fact that it is (1) not transitory but a permanently held conviction; (2) is a force derived from knowledge and experience; (3) that as knowledge and experience are possible in only a very restricted field, the action of true conscience is limited to THAT field, and (4) the challenge that conscience evokes is never destructive, but on the contrary aims to strengthen the structure of the society in which it is active.

Authority is free and strong when it resists the pressure of transient opinion and at the same time recognises conscience as a legitimate force in even its quietest and most obscure subjects.

Let us remember when we feel ourselves aghast at the present disclosures of the workings of Spiritual Absolutism, that things were not always thus in our Church, that they have become such in modern times. That the revelation of the spiritual terror that lies behind the façade of Roman Catholic Unity is part of the present revelation of the whole horror of modern thought, as distinct from medieval thought.

As far as this goes, everybody's hands are red. Behind the much vaunted 'unity' and stability of the Roman Catholic Church lie the conditions of spiritual and physical terror touched on in this book. Behind the 'success' of Communism lie the purges of the past. Behind Hitler's 'indestructible' Third Reich lay the concentration camps. Behind our 'victory' in world war two lie the betrayal of Poland and the smoke of Hiroshima.

So, therefore, we are all guilty and should confess ourselves as such. This Modern world of ours, developed since the Renaissance with such a vaunting of man's powers, has produced, on all fronts, unspeakable horrors, betrayal of humanity itself and death on an unprecedented scale.

That those aspects of the Roman Catholic Church that are modern and human and erroneous should be coming in for the same shaking and sifting to which all modern institutions have been subjected is only right and to be expected.

It is on the ashes of this modern world that the new world order must be built and it is we who are called to start the building now. We have to discover anew the foundations of justice and right order. History itself supplies all the lessons we need to know. Our major building tool must be that supplied by a rightly informed conscience. The power to achieve this must come from the power of the living God within us, who has said to us that He will come and pitch His tabernacle amongst us and that we are to be His people and He is to be our God.

And we should be of good courage when we undertake this work, for do we not have it on His own authority that in this work He will Himself be engaged? For 'behold' saith the Lord, 'I MAKE ALL THINGS NEW'.

The following authorities on the Middle Ages are the ones chiefly drawn upon in this chapter:

Otto Gierke (translated by F. W. Maitland): *Political Theories of The Middle Ages*. Cambridge U.P., 1900.

Professor C. H. McIlwain of Harvard: *The Growth of Political Thought in the West*. Macmillan, New York. P.197.

Professor Paul Vinogradoff: *Roman Law in Medieval Europe*. Lecture IV, Harpers, 1909

Printed by The Murray Printing Company
Bound by The Haddon Craftsmen, Inc.
HARPER & ROW, PUBLISHERS, INCORPORATED